I0199781

"Filled with stories—many of them personal—and undergirded by Scripture, Woodworth carefully, biblically, systematically, and pastorally detangles believers from the sin of partiality to fully and unabashedly embrace other persons made in God's image. And leaving nothing to chance, Woodworth provides discussion questions for each chapter to further help with liberating us from this partiality entanglement to freely, warmly, and impartially embrace *all* neighbors."

—LUKE B. BOBO
Director of Strategic Partnerships, Made to Flourish

"*Playing Favorites* is a helpful reminder of the call to see others not through human eyes of division but as beings made in the image of God reflecting the beauty of diversity. Woodworth recounts for us that prejudice is not what bad people have but is a condition that all people have. . . . May we have the courage, humility, and intentionality to take the lessons in this timely text to heart."

—TODD ALLEN
Vice President of Diversity, Messiah College

"Woodworth shows us how powerfully the gospel bridges the gaps in our hearts that keep us from loving one another. This book is an invitation to engage our neighbors with grace-fused intention—moving toward the marginalized and disenfranchised with the powerful and transformational love of Christ."

—JEREMY CASELLA
Nashville Singer/Songwriter and Recording Artist

"This book is a welcome addition to our culture's conversation about racial inequity and personal responsibility. Biblically grounded in timeless wisdom, Woodworth's words are as practical as they are pastoral. A good read for anyone, but especially helpful to those Christians who are looking for something that is not judgmental and offers a solid biblical approach to today's most challenging and important issue."

—DEAN WEAVER
Stated Clerk, Evangelical Presbyterian Church

"In Playing Favorites, Woodworth offers a theological vision for navigating multicultural contexts with wisdom and grace that avoids the ideological pitfalls common in our cultural moment. It's rooted in decades of ministry experience and informed by a careful reading of the Bible. In a time flooded with polarizing opinions, we need more gospel-centered sages like Rodger to guide us toward God's glorious vision for the church."

—AUSTIN GOHN
author of *A Restless Age*

"As Americans, we often like to refer to ourselves as color-blind. Woodworth points out that this is far from the truth. Woodworth does an excellent job of . . . weaving together personal experiences and societal research in presenting the problem of discrimination and prejudice. Fortunately, he does not stop with the problem but . . . guides us as we begin the journey of overcoming our prejudices and building bridges. It is with great pleasure that I recommend Playing Favorites."

—WAYNE GORDON
Pastor, Lawndale Community Church

"Born of his lifelong reading of the word and the world, Woodworth enters into the perennial problem of prejudice, a challenge for the church in every century and every culture. We stumble over ourselves, more often than not living with wounds of class and race that keep us from a deeper, truer unity. Playing Favorites offers another way to live, both a critique of what is, and a vision for what should be. A book for all who long to see and hear the world as it someday will be."

—STEVEN GARBER

author of *Visions of Vocation: Common Grace for the Common Good*

Playing Favorites

Playing Favorites

Overcoming Our Prejudices
to Bridge the Cultural Divide

Rodger Woodworth

WIPF & STOCK · Eugene, Oregon

PLAYING FAVORITES
Overcoming Our Prejudices to Bridge the Cultural Divide

Copyright © 2021 Rodger Woodworth. All rights reserved. Except for brief quotations in critical publications or reviews, no part of this book may be reproduced in any manner without prior written permission from the publisher. Write: Permissions, Wipf and Stock Publishers, 199 W. 8th Ave., Suite 3, Eugene, OR 97401.

Wipf & Stock
An Imprint of Wipf and Stock Publishers
199 W. 8th Ave., Suite 3
Eugene, OR 97401

www.wipfandstock.com

PAPERBACK ISBN: 978-1-6667-3042-5
HARDCOVER ISBN: 978-1-6667-2195-9
EBOOK ISBN: 978-1-6667-2196-6

OCTOBER 14, 2021

Biblical quotations are used by permission from the New Living Translation, copyright @1996, 2004, 2015 by Tyndale House Publishers, Inc. All rights reserved.

I want to dedicate this book to our first son-in-law and my former assistant pastor, Matt Smith, who went to be with our Lord far too soon. He showed me that with the love of Christ there was no cultural or racial divide that could not be bridged.

Contents

Acknowledgments

I OWE A DEEP and sincere note of gratitude to my wife Wende, whose unconditional love has made me better at everything I do. To our children, B. J. and Brooke, who inspire and amaze me with their godly character, and to Katrina and Jeremy; no one but God could have provided such loving spouses. To our grandchildren, Kyra, Maddie, Elena, Grace, Alex, Zach, Jackson, Eli, and Millie, thank you for the incredible joy you bring to me, which among other things encourages me to write.

Thank you to the numerous parishioners I had the privilege of pastoring and to the communities where I was called to plant a church. You taught me so much by the way you loved me. I also owe so much to the many African American pastors and leaders who patiently mentored me and befriended me. To Gram and Rev., Drs. James and Betty Robinson, who upon retirement came and sat under this white man's preaching and quietly supported and loved Wende and me. To the late Rev. Maurice Doss, I thank him for our weekly lunches that often went into the late afternoons. I miss his wisdom and partnership in helping others understand true racial reconciliation.

Introduction

MOST OF US LIKE to assume that we're enlightened, tolerant, and unprejudiced people. Unfortunately, a study in 2010 revealed many of us have a hidden bias against anyone with a foreign accent. According to a summary of the study in the *Wall Street Journal*, "The further from native-sounding an accent is, the harder we have to work, and the less trustworthy we perceive the information to be." It gets worse: "Researchers found that the heavier the accent, the more skeptical participants became."[1] In other words, if it sounds like you're not from around here, our suspicion alarm goes off. Our bias about others isn't based on their character; it's based on the fact that they talk "different."

The researchers assure us that we're not necessarily racist. Evidently, our brains are lazy. According to researchers, our brains simply prefer the path of least resistance. In fact, additional research reveals that our brains tell us to perceive anyone different than us as a threat.[2] We are all susceptible to ethnocentrism. People are more comfortable with others of the same race, tribe, and religion. When Black and white Americans were shown photos of the other race, their brains' centers of fear and anger were triggered so quickly that they were not even conscious of their response.[3] All of this is a nice way to say that, despite our best intentions, we all have

1. McClesky, "Accentuating Bias."
2. Amodio, "Neuroscience of Prejudice and Stereotyping."
3. Wilson, *Social Conquest of Earth,* 60.

our prejudices, preferences, and priorities. In biblical terms, we show partiality toward people who resemble us; we play favorites.

John Ortberg thought of this tendency to favor people almost every time he flew on an airplane.[4] The first-class passengers were served gourmet food by their own flight attendants while those in coach got a handful of peanuts. The first-class passengers had room to stretch and sleep; those in coach sat close enough to be making out in the back row of a movie theater. On almost every flight, once the plane was under way, a curtain got drawn to separate the two compartments. It was not to be violated; it was like the Berlin Wall or the veil that separated the Court of the Gentiles from the holy of holies in the temple at Jerusalem. The curtain was a reminder throughout the flight that some people were first class and some were not. The airline wanted everyone in the Court of the Gentiles to know that they were not allowed to use the facilities in the holy of holies, even though there was one restroom for eight people up front and two restrooms for several hundred of those in the back. The curtain stood for a tendency deep inside our fallen nature to favor some and exclude others. In this act of partiality we divide the world up into us and them.

Authors Arne Roets and Alain Van Hiel of Ghent University in Belgium write, "Social categories are useful to reduce complexity, but the problem is that we also assign some properties to these categories. This can lead to prejudice and stereotyping." The result is that when we meet someone new, we evaluate and judge that one based on his or her categorization. Roets writes, "You say, 'he's part of this group, so he's probably like this.'" Roets concludes, "To reduce prejudice, we first have to acknowledge that it often satisfies some basic need to have quick answers and stable knowledge people rely on to make sense of the world."[5]

Paul wrote to the Corinthian church that "we have stopped evaluating others from a human point of view" (2 Cor 5:16). The church had become seers instead of believers; they were seeing

4. Ortberg, "Our Tendency to Exclude."

5. Roets, in Roets and Van Hiel, "Allport's Prejudiced Personality Today," 349–54.

others from the categories of a worldly perspective. They were measuring them based on the distinctions of their world—male and female, Jew and Greek, slave and free. However, Paul shares that those who become Christians become new persons. They are not the same anymore, for the old life is gone and a new life has begun! This new humanity is only made possible by the blood of Christ and the grace of a God who shows no partiality, who hung out with women, Samaritans, lepers, tax collectors, and an assortment of sinners.

When we apply our yardsticks to evaluate others and ask God to bless our methods of measuring, we nullify God's grace. No wonder so much of the unbelieving world has stopped responding to the gospel. Instead we should bring our dueling yardsticks to the cross and ask God to crucify them. From much of the world's point of view, life is about power and control, but at the cross we should surrender that control, including our power over the measurement of others. The way out of the garden of evaluating others by what the world thinks about them, and into the new humanity of God's kingdom, is surrendering our yardsticks.

President Lyndon B. Johnson reportedly said to a young Bill Moyers: "If you can convince the lowest white man he's better than the best colored man, he won't notice you're picking his pocket. Hell, give him somebody to look down on, and he'll empty his pockets for you." Yet the apostle Paul taught a different worldview to follow, that in humility we are to count others as more significant than ourselves (Phil. 2:3). Even those who are uneducated or jobless, too different or too disagreeable, are to be counted not just as equals but as more significant than us—the exact opposite of feeling superior. Paul's point is not about what others are but what we count others to be. The focus is not on how well they speak, how much money they make, the color of their skin, or their political views. The focus is: will we count them as worthy of our friendship, encouragement, or help? Will we take thought not just for our interests but for theirs? Will we take time to get to know them, help build them up, and even learn from them?

How does this orientation to the other, this coming together from divergent directions, happen? How can we stop playing favorites and overcome our culture's divisions? The answer is humility, literally, lowliness. A humility that comes from recognizing the overwhelming, moment by moment, act of God's grace in our lives, promised for eternity. Imagine how different our world could be if we actually counted others as more significant: maybe a more civil political discourse, a less segregated Sunday church, a little less racism and classism. Just imagine the possibilities.

In Miroslav Volf's book *Exclusion and Embrace,* his idea of "double vision" seems to be one of the more important instructions on embracing and loving others who are different than us, including our enemies. Volf says we must allow others and those with whom we are in conflict to "re-adjust our perspective as we take into account their perspective." This again takes great humility, as it requires the recognition that we have not cornered the market on truth. Our reversal of perspectives is what keeps us from perverting justice or what Amos calls "turning justice into poison" (Amos 6:12). This theological exploration of identity, otherness, and reconciliation is deep but practical for embracing God's impartiality. Double vision involves a self-giving love whose "weakness is stronger than social concern and foolishness is wiser than rational thought."[6]

I had the opportunity to spend a month in South Africa a few years after apartheid, including time with Desmond Tutu and a few members of the Truth and Reconciliation Commission. We heard stories of people who came before the commission, like those of Mrs. Calata and her daughter. Mrs. Calata's husband had been an advocate for Black South Africans in rural communities. Because of his work, he'd been arrested, detained, and tortured by the police numerous times. But one day he disappeared. On the front page of the newspaper, Mrs. Calata saw a photograph of her husband's car on fire. She cried so loudly during the hearing which described the autopsy's report about his torture that the commission had to be adjourned. When they reconvened, Mrs. Calata's

6. Volf, *Exclusion and Embrace,* 28.

daughter testified. Years had gone by, and she was now a young woman. She pleaded with the commission to discover who had killed her father. But she was not crying out because she wanted vengeance or justice. Instead she said to the commission, "We want to forgive, but we don't know whom to forgive." Eventually members of the police confessed to the crime. Rather than continue the endless cycle of hatred and exclusion, Mrs. Calata and her daughter forgave the men who tortured and killed their husband and father, because that's what Christ's people do.

Forgiveness doesn't mean we don't care about justice. What it means is that we leave justice and vengeance in God's hands. He alone can judge rightly. Our job, as citizens of God's kingdom on earth, is to move from being a people of exclusion to a people of embrace, forgiving others just as God, in Christ, has forgiven us.

Humility, forgiveness, and seeing others as more significant than ourselves are a few of the ways we begin to embrace the impartiality of God and overcome our culture's divisions. We begin to stand out from those entrenched in their political, racial, and even religious foxholes, where verbal salvos are thrown at those who disagree with them. We become more like citizens of God's kingdom on earth or what sociologists call third-culture people. F. L. Casmir defines third culture as "the construction of a mutually beneficial interactive environment in which individuals from two [or more] different cultures can function in a way beneficial to all involved."[7] Third-culture people have a cultural sensibility and intelligence to embrace and bridge all kinds of differences. They have a unique awareness and appreciation of the richness and value of different worldviews and cultures. They don't engage in culture wars, they celebrate cultural diversity and look to love, learn, and serve in any context, even when it may be uncomfortable or painful.

I grew up in a working-class family in a rural, small-town setting. It was an all-white culture. My exposure to other ethnic or racial lifestyles was limited to that rare encounter during my athletic endeavors. I couldn't even superficially say I knew a Black

7. Casmir, ed., *Ethics*, 92.

person. It wasn't until basic training that I came face to face with my very dark-skinned African American drill sergeant. Strangely, I was drawn to this man and worked hard to earn his trust and approval. We even had some man-to-man conversations about life, at least as man to man as you can have with your drill sergeant. Just prior to graduation from basic, a serious racial fight broke out among members of my barracks. While I didn't participate, I was present, and the resulting injuries to some of those involved in the ruckus ended in everyone being brought before the company commander. Nothing happened to me except a good reprimand from my military authority. However, my drill sergeant was present, and I was embarrassed to have been observing this mini riot. Somehow I felt I had betrayed him. At that moment I realized how much I had come to respect and appreciate this Black man, this Vietnam veteran, this person so culturally different from me. Something had begun to change in me, a new awareness and a surprising interest in cultural diversity.

Several years later our young family moved into the city, for less than spiritual reasons, or at least I thought. We had found an area where we could afford our first house, but as it turned out it was where I would get my call to vocational ministry. It has since been nearly forty years of life and ministry in an urban context, planting and pastoring interracial churches while learning to love and serve a diverse neighborhood. Along this journey, one of several African American pastors, whom I had ask to mentor me, began referring to me as bicultural. I had become adept at moving between the culture of the white suburban church and the Black urban community. I felt at home in both worlds as I worked at drawing their respective cultures together. It was rarely easy, and I made my share of mistakes, but it seemed to line up with God's will for his coming kingdom and his loving nature to be impartial.

In 1993, William Pannell wrote his insightful but controversial book, *The Coming Race Wars?: A Cry for Reconciliation*. At the end of his final chapter, he writes: "Black people and white people still view each other warily and from a distance. Other ethnic groups have been sucked into the vortex of the storm and all of us for some time to come will be struggling to get past the temptation to avoid caring about each other one way or the other."[8] That statement is as true now as it was then. Even though the Bible says that, as Christians, we are all one in Christ Jesus, despite racial differences, the temptation to play favorites and avoid spanning the racial and cultural chasm is ever present. In my continued commitment to the work of reconciliation, I hope this book will encourage and instruct our faith journey to overcome our prejudices to bridge the cultural divide.

8. Pannell, *Coming Race Wars*, 143.

Chapter 1

God's Nature of Impartiality

How often, when I began to lose confidence in my ability to live and minister in our multi-cultural community, I clothed myself in the pride of being a white Anglo-Saxon Protestant. Richard Lovelace, in his book entitled *Dynamics of a Spiritual Life,* wrote: "Men who are not secure in Christ cast about for spiritual life-preservers with which to support their confidence, and in their frantic search they not only cling to the shreds of ability and righteousness they find in themselves, but they fix upon their race, their membership in a party, their familiar social and ecclesiastical patterns, and their culture as a means of self-recommendation."[1]

In these uncertain and chaotic times, people are putting on the armor of their respective political parties while throwing insults at the other side. Deaths at the hands of police have deepened the racial divides. The megachurch has thrived on the pride of people's identity in their membership of a successful church. Anxiety and insecurity can lead to the hubris desire of asserting the righteousness of our own group while criticizing others.

All of this reeks of the Tower of Babel, "a time when the whole world spoke a single language" and "began to take advantage of their common language and political unity" (Gen 11:1, 6). The people were striving for a unity that would give them security

1. Lovelace, *Dynamics of Spiritual Life,* 198–99.

and make a name for them. While Jesus tells us that unity will be the major way outsiders will know God sent his Son, it is a unity of Christians who are different from one another, culturally, racially, and economically, that contains the true glory of God. God confirmed this at Pentecost, when he began to reverse the curse of Babel by showing that his Holy Spirit can overcome the linguistic and ethnic barriers we erect.

For ages, people have retreated into the security of familiar customs and cultures and have regarded differences as something to avoid. These prejudices and preferences, according to Tim Keller, are a form of self-righteousness, a way to feel acceptable and worthwhile on our own merits. We do this when we begin to convince ourselves that our race, our tradition, or our politics are superior to others. If we are to really embody the gospel to the world around us, we must have a bias towards being third culture, a culture that benefits and reconciles both sides of a division. We can only do that when our security and identity is fully in Christ and not our cultural heritage, an identity that embraces God's impartiality.

Romans 2:11 says, "For there is no partiality with God," and Deuteronomy 10:17 states, "He is the great God . . . who shows no partiality and cannot be bribed." These are just a few of many verses threaded throughout Scripture that affirm God's impartiality, with other Scriptures revealing our tendency to do just the opposite. In the Deuteronomy text, the Hebrew word for impartiality means God does not lift his face. In other words, God does not regard the face of people; it is his very nature to show no favoritism. This does not mean God is colorblind, as some like to say. One Black pastor said to me, "Don't tell me you don't see color, otherwise how do you describe me to the police." The original designer of our skin pigmentation does see color, but it does not affect his high regard for each of us. To reflect God's universal impartiality, we are told in the previous verse to stop being stubborn or stiff necked, but rather love the aliens and foreigners among you, love those whose skin color is different from yours.

The apostle James is greatly concerned about how our love for one another can be affected by attitudes of superiority based on differences. He writes in his letter: "Suppose someone comes into your meeting dressed in fancy clothes and expensive jewelry, and another comes in who is poor and dressed in dirty clothes. If you give special attention and a good seat to the rich person, but you say to the poor one, 'You can stand over there, or else sit on the floor'—well, doesn't this partiality show that your judgments are guided by evil motives?" (Jas 2:2–4). In James 2:9, the author uses a Greek word for partiality or discrimination that literally means "to regard the face" of another, the exact opposite of God's impartiality. And if that regard results in favoring "some people over others, you are committing a sin" (Jas 2:9).

Why is favoritism a sin? According to James, it is a contradiction to having faith in Christ. Favoritism and faith don't mix, and they include all kinds of impartial acts. When we show partiality we discriminate, we make distinctions, and we set ourselves up as judges with evil thoughts. I heard Lew Gervais, director of Pressing Onward, share the story of Bill, a wild-haired, recent college believer, whose wardrobe was jeans and a T-shirt with holes in it. Across from campus was a well-dressed, very conservative church. One Sunday, Bill decided to go there. He walked in late and shoeless. The sanctuary was packed. Bill heads down the aisle, looking for a seat. Having nearly reached the pulpit, he realizes there are no empty seats, so he sits down on the carpet. The congregation is feeling uncomfortable. Then from the back of the church, a gray-haired elder in a three-piece suit starts walking toward Bill with a cane. The worshipers didn't expect a man in his eighties to understand some college kid on the floor. With all eyes focused on the developing drama, the minister waits to begin his sermon until the elder does what he has to do. The elderly man drops his cane on the floor and with great difficulty lowers himself to sit next to Bill. "What I'm about to preach," the minister begins, "you'll never remember. What you've just seen, you'll never forget."

Playing favorites or discriminating is the same as being double minded and unstable in our belief. James uses the same

Greek word for doubt and discriminate. When we discriminate, like doubting and having a divided loyalty, we become like "a wave of the sea that is blown and tossed by the wind" (Jas 1:6).

Have you ever seen a statue or picture of Lady Justice? Often found on the top or in front of a courthouse is a statue of this robed woman representing justice. She has a balance in her left hand, to show that justice weighs cases to see what is right. In her right hand is a sword, to show that justice has the authority of government on her side. But she also has a blindfold across her eyes, to show that justice should be objective, without "regarding the face" of people. Cases of justice should be decided regardless of the identity, money, power, or position of a person. This is what it means to be impartial. Ultimately, impartiality is a feature of heavenly wisdom, because this is an attribute of God. Again, the Bible makes clear that God is impartial. In our country and in others, the powerful and wealthy are often favored by the legal system, but that is not true of God. He treats everyone the same, whether the person is an orphan, widow, or an alien.

James continues in his epistle to challenge his readers with the question of which is more valuable: to be poor financially but rich in faith or to be like an unbelieving rich person who exploits the poor (Jas 2:5–7). The apostle is asking whether this is true in our lives; do we favor people who are rich and famous, or do we favor a faith that is rich?

I once had the unusual experience of running into a well-known actor at my racquetball club. He was in town filming a movie and had come to get some exercise. We ended up on the courts next to each other and engaged in some polite conversation. When he discovered I was a pastor, surprisingly his interest peaked. He had been meeting with a pastor in L.A. seeking to discover how Christianity fit into the world's religions. I quickly offered to provide some similar conversations, and before I knew it, I was given his pseudonym at the hotel where he was staying and was asked to call him. We talked on only one occasion, but he offered to have me visit their filming site. Unfortunately, he called me back that morning to share that the filming location had changed and he was not sure where they would be that day. Since the coming Sunday was Easter, I took the bold move to invite him to our little multiracial church, with no expectation of that happening. I told no one about this except my wife and our head usher, just in case the unimaginable happened. Fifteen minutes into our service, our usher came up to whisper in my ear, "He is here." Like most churches on Easter Sunday, we were packed and our ushers did what James warns about; they gave our famous guest and his two friends "special attention and a good seat." I confess I too got caught up in this favoritism, and with permission I introduced our venerable and very wealthy guest. Needless to say, our greeting time was a little longer than usual.

Now I could find all kinds of appropriate justification for our church's response. After all, the chasm between the lifestyle of our working poor neighborhood and the stardom of our new visitor was significant, to say the least. We couldn't really blame ourselves for being so taken by this once-in-a-lifetime encounter. Yet, regardless of our reasons, this brief event had revealed a tendency in all of us to favor some people over others.

Favoritism has a broader reach then an encounter with the rich and famous. Our materialism can result in economic favoritism, and racism is rooted in an ethnic partiality. The principle of favoritism is based on the worldly values of social status, heritage, race, and appearances, and not only opposes the grace of God but breaks the law of loving our neighbor as ourselves. This requires us to love anyone, regardless of wealth, position, abilities, education, or dress. To ignore the sin of favoritism is to ignore the whole law of God. Imagine hanging over a ten-story building holding onto a chain. How many pieces of chain need to break before you fall to your death?

Favoritism is also the sin of extending special favors to some for self-serving purposes.

How often we treat relationships as an opportunity to accomplish a business-related or personal goal! In the process, we learn how to impress people with our success and evaluate others by the marks of their success or failures, resulting in the fear of exposing our own weaknesses. We hide our imperfections, we lack mercy, and friendships become self-serving and even competitive. Our relationships should be competitive free zones. "Instead of maneuvering for the best possible advantage, we give ourselves to one another for the sake of Christ."[2]

James attempts to draw a contrast between God's attitude towards people whom we judge do not measure up and our own attitudes. We make human distinctions based on sinful motives rather than on God's holy impartiality, based on his word. The problem is we fail to realize we are those people. The truth is we are like the ones whom we do not favor or we discriminate against. Most of us are one paycheck, one divorce, one drug-addicted kid, one mental health diagnosis, one serious illness, one sexual assault, one drinking binge, one night of unprotected sex, or one affair away from being "those people"—the ones we don't trust, the ones we pity, the ones we don't let our children play with, the ones bad things happen to, the ones we don't want living next door.[3]

In the midst of our political and racial disunity these days, I have found some optimism when Paul writes in Ephesians 1:10, "At the right time he [God] will bring everything together under the authority of Christ." The Greek phrase translated as "everything together" is used only one other time in the New Testament, "For the commandments . . . are all summed up [everything together] in this one commandment: 'Love your neighbor as yourself'" (Rom 13:19). All the commandments are brought together in "love your neighbor as yourself." This summation of everything, this bringing together of everything, this uniting of everything, finds its place under the authority of Christ and in the command to love our neighbors.

Regardless of future elections or continued racial injustice, some day in this already but not yet future of Christ's lordship, all things in heaven and earth will be united. That means no more discord, all things will be brought into a meaningful relationship, no more fragmentation, no more frustration, no more divisions,

2. Webster, *Finding Spiritual Direction*, 75.
3. Morgan, *Beauty of Broken*, 25.

and no more derision. Things don't add up right now, but in the future, they will all be summed up, they will all be brought together in unity. The lion will lie down with the lamb, racial tensions will disappear, and, yes, even the Democrats and the Republicans will embrace across the dividing walls of hostility.

This coming unity, according to Ephesians, was preceded by God choosing us in Christ and adopting us into his family. This was not for our individual benefit but as a corporate one, "for the benefit of the church" (Eph 1:22). In other words, the church should be not only a model of unity but a catalyst for unity in the divided world in which we live. Our first allegiance is to the Lordship of the Christ who has guaranteed us a future unity of all things, not our political party. That optimism should call us to walk in that unity and not participate in disunity.

In the book *Against All Odds,* the authors' research on the struggle for racial integration in religious organizations reveals that most of those who are part of an ethnically diverse church would never consider going back to a homogeneous model.[4] Why? When we ignore God's impartiality and play favorites, our lives become impoverished, when we do not engage and reflect the nature of God's multiethnic kingdom and his impartiality. Our understanding of God's kingdom is limited when everyone's struggles are the same; it limits our knowledge of God's sovereignty and providence. When there is a diversity of cultures, economics, race, and politics, we experience God's grace in ways that may be unfamiliar to us. Our prejudices are revealed, and we are stretched to love those who may not love us back. Not unlike our God, who loves us unconditionally without getting back the love he deserves. Let us give thanks that the Creator and Sustainer of the universe does not play favorites.

---

4. Christerson et al., *Against All Odds.*

Chapter 2

Jesus's Creation of Oneness

THE 1992 FILM A *River Runs through It,* based on the autobiographical novel of Norman Maclean, chronicles two brothers coming of age in early twentieth-century Missoula, Montana.[1] The boys grew up under the stern tutelage of their minister father, played by Tom Skerritt. This preacher teaches his sons about life, grace, and love through the art of fly-fishing. As the boys mature and follow very different paths (one straight and narrow, the other wild), they find that fishing is the one bond that still draws them together as adults. Thus the title was not a description of the land as much as it was a description of a recurring theme in their lives. When all else failed, they could always go back to the river and bond around their love of fly-fishing.

The description of a recurring theme for Christians today, as we may struggle with difficult relationships and cultural divisions, could be called "a cross runs through it." When the political and social rhetoric draw us into sinful responses and we retreat behind the walls of our brand of homogeneous protection, we can go to the cross. We ask for forgiveness and embrace the One who died for us there. It can be so easy today to barricade ourselves behind a wall of hostility or indifference and join our favorite group to throw things at the opposition. Have we lost the power of the gospel to a

1. Redford, dir., *River Runs through It.*

nationalism that threatens to replace the cross with a flag? We can love those who don't measure up to our cultural expectations only because Christ died on the cross for our failure to bridge the very dividing barriers we have erected.

Sometimes we like building walls; in fact, human beings have always been preoccupied with such a task. In the first century, the Roman emperor Hadrian built a seventy-five-mile wall across Roman Britain. In the 1870s, Argentina built a line of trenches and watchtowers called the Zanja de Alsina to protect Buenos Aires from invasion by indigenous peoples. The Berlin Wall went up in 1961, dividing East from West for almost thirty years. In 1975, South Africa built a 3,500-volt electric fence dubbed the Snake of Fire to keep the civil war in Mozambique from spilling over into the frontier. In the middle of the night in August 2006, Italian officials constructed a steel wall around Via Anelli, a run-down neighborhood known for drug trafficking and prostitution. And then there is our own country's attempt to build a wall on our southern border as part of an immigration policy, reportedly to keep out the prostitutes and drug dealers.

Walls don't just divide us. They also can make us sick. After the Berlin Wall went up, East German psychiatrists observed that the Berlin Wall caused mental illness, rage, dejection, and addiction. The closer to the physical wall people lived, the more acute their disorders. The only cure for "wall disease" was to bring the wall down. Sure enough, in 1990, psychiatrists noted the "emotional liberation" felt after November 9, 1989, when the wall finally fell. Thousands of jubilant Germans climbed the wall, wept, embraced each other atop the concrete, and proceeded to tear the wall down with joyful abandon.[2]

Ephesians 2:14 says Jesus did what those Germans did: "He broke down the wall of hostility that separated us." And Jesus's whole purpose was to create "one new people." The word for "new" that Paul uses here is the idea of an invention. It not the new car in the showroom; it's the first car ever invented. In other words, Christ died to create something the world had never seen: two

2. Di Cintio, *Walls*, 10–12.

groups of people, Jews and Gentiles, who hated each other, coming together to be reconciled. There was no model or paradigm for two formerly hostile ethnicities doing life with one another, sharing meals and worshipping together. Sadly, instead of tearing down our walls with joyful abandon, many are resurrecting the walls of exclusion, in our politics, our neighborhoods, our churches, and our hearts.

In order to grow, lobsters have to rid themselves of their old, hard, protective shell and grow a new, larger one. They need the shell to protect them from being torn apart, yet when they grow, the old shell must be abandoned. If they did not abandon it, the old shell would soon become their prison and finally their casket. This process of shedding an old shell is called molting. They do this about twenty-five times in the first five years of life and once a year after they become adults. It is an ugly, messy process. Under the pressure, the old, hard, protective shell cracks. Then the lobster lies on its side, flexes its muscles, and pulls itself from the cracked shell. For a short time, between the leaving of the old and the hardening of a new one, the lobster is naked and very vulnerable to the elements.

We are not so different from lobsters. To change and grow, to tear down our walls of excluding others, we must shed our shells, such as our cultural worldview on which we've come to depend. Our cultural worldview is those unconscious beliefs, patterns, values, and myths that affect everything we do and say. All forms of Christianity have been affected by cultural prejudices. The Western Enlightenment has blinded some of us to the spirit world, while African superstition has distorted others' view of Christianity.

Peter says as Christians we are a "holy nation," literally, we are a new ethnicity (1 Pet 2:9). All Christians, while staying connected to our cultures of origin, must get enough distance to identify and shed our shells of cultural idols. To do that, we need the help of other cultures to honestly critique our own cultural view of the world. Christianity does not replace our cultural identity with some other culture but rather converts it; it transforms us in the soil of our respective cultures. This process is called discipleship—leaving the old and waiting for the hardening of the new—and this can leave us feeling naked and vulnerable. It means being so committed to Christ that when he bids us to follow, we will risk change, grow, and leave our cultural shells behind.

I have always had a vision for a church that is racially, economically, and generationally diverse. A church where our diverse identities do not disappear, but where those identities bow to the cross of Christ that runs through every relationship. A church whose light shines into the rising darkness of hostility and racism, as well as the growing indifference of our secular age. The only way that light shines is with a cross running through it. It is only the cross that starts with alienation and ends with reconciliation, that moves people from exclusion to embrace and ends a system of injustice that makes everyone equal. It is the cross that creates a third culture, a new humanity out of previously hostile and alienated people. God gave his Son not that we might become better people but rather a brand-new humanity.

The divide between Jews and gentiles was no small thing. It was huge, it was complex, and it was first and foremost religious. The Jews had the inside track on the one true God, and Jewish Christians knew God's Son, the one true Messiah, Jesus the Christ. These latecoming gentiles were required to jump through the appropriate ecclesiastical hoops. You might call it a kind of ceremonial hazing to join the religious fraternity. The divide was also cultural. Customs and traditions such as circumcision, dietary laws, and rules of cleanliness had to be followed in order to be included. All of these things had a purpose at one time, to set the Jewish people apart from other nations and to draw them closer to God. Now they were being used to create walls of exclusion. Lastly, the divide was racial. The Jews had the right bloodlines, going back to Jacob and Isaac, not Esau and Ishmael. That divide continues in the Middle East conflict today. While at times these wars appear to be more tribal than racial and religious, they can be historically traced back to the conflict between Isaac and Ishmael (Gen 16).

This division between Jews and gentiles was as big as any divide we have today, between Black and white, political parties, economic status, or any groups that point fingers at each other. Decades ago, Ann Landers wrote a column in which she tried to depict what the earth would be like after a nuclear war. And she asked all of her readers to clip the article and to send it to the White House. The President wrote her a letter about two weeks later in which he acknowledged that he had received over two hundred clippings. But then he went on to suggest, "I think you sent them to the wrong place. They should have been sent to the Kremlin." The problem is with those other guys.[3] That's always the problem with reconciling differences; it's those other guys.

Here is what God did in Christ to all the division and hostility between these two groups.

He brought those who were on the outside in through Christ's work on the cross. He ended the system of exclusion, and he reconciled both these former enemies through Christ's sacrificial death. Through the blood of Christ, God brought outsiders in, ended the systems of exclusion and reconciled these two hostile groups (Eph 2:15–17). In other words, to be accepted into this new humanity, it was no longer based on your ethnic background or keeping the law, it was based on the grace of God and Christ's work on the cross.

So why do we still have such hostility and division in our politics, our race relations, and our culture in general? Why do we still erect fences around our neighbors who are different from us? Why are Sunday mornings still the most segregated hour of the week? Sociologists define a multiethnic church as one in which no single ethnicity makes up more than 80 percent of those who attend. There are roughly 300,000 congregations in the U.S. today—Christian, Jewish, Muslim, and Mormon—who gather to worship. When you apply the standard for being a multiethnic congregation, about 16 percent qualify; and when you apply it to Christian churches, it is 24 percent for Catholics, 11 percent for mainline Protestants, and 23 percent for evangelical churches. While all of these statistics are an improvement from 1998 to this

---

3. Thielemann, "Hark! the Herald Angels."

most recent report,[4] it is still a long way from God's purpose to create one new people. We still have divisions and fences, because even our religious institutions have not modeled a true picture of unity in diversity.

Brenda Salter McNeil in *The Heart of Racial Justice* writes there are two primary models that have been used by American Christians to overcome the racial and ethnic divide.[5] The first is the relational model; make a friend with someone from a different race or ethnicity. This was the Promise Keepers' approach in the 1990s. I always felt sorry for Black men at such events, as hundreds of white men lined up to give them a hug. This model has its strengths, because it is a simple way to get started, especially since most white evangelicals understand the gospel from an individualistic worldview. And it's always nice to be able to say at the right time, "I have a Black friend." The problem is this model does not take into account the history and the resulting structures of racism and the personal rage and hurt a lifetime of injustice has reaped. I can learn about an innocent Black person being followed around in a department store out of concern she or he is going to shoplift, but I will never have to experience it.

The second model that McNeil suggests has been used is the institutional change paradigm: redistribute wealth and power, using ethnic and racial quotas, job training, community organizing, and school reforms. These are great things if they also encourage personal responsibility, empower, people with knowledge, and take into account systemic injustices and racism. The problem with this model is it can reduce all relationships to the issue of power and control. However, the kingdom of God is not about competition for power.

We need a balance of the best from both of these models. We need relationships that cross racial and cultural divides, and we need institutional change that brings justice for all. However, we cannot seem to get there, because we lack a robust theology of the cross running through our individual relationships and our

4. Emerson, "Released," paras. 8–9.

5. McNeil, in McNeil and Richardson, *Heart of Racial Justice*, 47–50.

institutional reforms. Every time we move towards relationships and reforms that would bring reconciliation and justice, walls of hostility and systems of exclusion are resurrected. We erect a fence around our heart every time we require someone to fit into our little box of cultural expectations before we forgive them or embrace them. We have our little cliques within our dominate culture to remind us of the existing walls that define those who are in and those who are not. There are our political ideologies and even our theological distinctives that further declare who we should or should not hang out with.

This is not unlike what the elder brother did to his brother the prodigal. After the younger brother left home with his inheritance and spent it all on wild living in a distant land, he returned home broken and repentant, ready to be treated as a hired servant. While the father raced out to embrace him, the older brother had built a fence around his heart. He no longer had space in his heart for such a blemished brother. His heart was actually filled with his younger brother's sin. The ways in which he felt his younger brother no longer fit into the family were now a wall of exclusion built out of his hostility. The one who squandered must repay. The one who disobeyed must do penance. For the older brother, you were either in or you were out, based on a set of rules. If you are out, there is no embrace, only exclusion (Luke 15:11–31). This happens in all sorts of ways in our schools, our churches, our neighborhoods, our politics, and our culture. Rules made to preserve social ties can also encourage self-righteousness and demonize outsiders.

We might ask at this point, doesn't God have rules? Are not people either in the kingdom of God or out of the kingdom? Yes, but here is one thing we forget. The rules have already been kept, fulfilled, and perfected. We are not in or out of God's kingdom because of how well we kept the rules. We are in the kingdom because we confessed we couldn't keep the rules and we trusted in the cross of Christ, where the punishment for breaking the rules was paid. We no longer live by the rules that exclude others, but we live through the One who kept the rules perfectly and who continually forgives us for breaking those high standards. We dare not rebuild the rules that exclude others.

The Jews interpreted the law to love their neighbors as a rule that had limits and that gave them permission to hate their enemies. Their understanding of love was driven by self-interest instead of God's self-sacrificial love on the cross. The goal of God's love is to embrace, not to exclude. Jesus's death on the cross brought a new and deeper understanding of what it means to be a part of God's kingdom, and it is unnatural. It is much more natural to abide by the principles of our secular world, which at best encourages us to ignore our enemies. However, the cross and the subsequent kingdom call us to an unnatural love, a love of enemies (Matt 5:43–48).

Jesus makes it clear that his Father loves his enemies every day. He gives sunlight and sends rain on the evil and the unjust. He has every right to withhold that common grace to the unrighteous, but instead he shows mercy and patience. Jesus said anyone can love a lover; even corrupt tax collectors did that much. How are you different from the pagans who are kind to their friends? The one thing that sets Christianity apart from all other religions is the love of Jesus Christ, of him who went patiently and obediently to the cross. The cross is the peculiar, extraordinary, unnatural hallmark of the Christian faith—a distinction that is displayed in the self-donating love of enemies, a love that prays even for those who persecute us.

Dietrich Bonhoeffer writes, "Through the medium of prayer we go to our enemy, stand by his side, and plead for him to God . . . so long as we pray for them, we are doing vicariously for them what they cannot do for themselves."[6] Can we imagine how things might be different if the politicians who claim to be followers of Christ prayed for their opponents; if pro-lifers prayed for Planned Parenthood; if Blacks, browns, and whites actually worshiped together in the same church every Sunday? It would be unnatural, but this self-donating love, this acting like children of our Father in heaven, just might allow the world to see more of God's coming kingdom. The cross running through our lives might even cause

6. Bonhoeffer, *Cost of Discipleship*, 149.

some in our secular world to seek the Divine and to become aware of the God-shaped hole in their lives.

To bring about Christ's new humanity, with a cross running through our relationships, takes intentionality. Jesus intentionally went to the cross to die. Paul intentionally went to the synagogue to preach to the Jews and went to the hall of Tyrannus and preached to the gentiles (Acts 19). Paul's intentionality created multiethnic relationships and churches. The challenge for most of us is that we limit our cross-cultural engagement to superficial relationships and events. Pulpit and choir exchanges between Black and white churches, attending Friendship Sunday at a church racially different from yours, or saying a friendly hello to your different neighbor are all good things but will fall short of the oneness Christ created on the cross. Even in our racially and economically diverse church, relationships often ended after people left the worship service to go home. Very few people crossed the racial barrier to invite others over for dinner. So when it came to establishing small groups, we had people sign up and then assigned each person a group to maintain economically and racially diverse gatherings, meeting in each other's homes. Every year we would reshuffle the deck, so everyone always had someone known from the previous year but also the opportunity to deepen a new relationship. This took intentionality and required a level of humility and sacrifice. We were also deliberate in holding off electing our first group of elders until we had an African American, as we were not going to have an all-white board. Both of these intentional decisions took a cross running through the lives of every person involved. It wasn't always easy, but it was glorious and honored Christ's death that dismantled our dividing walls to create one new humanity.

Chapter 3

Jesus's Work of Wall Breaking

IN AN ARTICLE FROM *World Magazine* entitled "Leaving Hate Behind," Sophia Lee offers a story of how God can break down the walls of racist ideology that are still prevalent today.

Tom Tarrants first questioned his extremist ideology while serving a 35-year sentence in prison for attempting to bomb a Jewish businessman's residence. Previously, Tarrants had avoided any literature that didn't support his white supremacist views. But with nothing to do in his tiny cell except think and read, he began devouring books about philosophy, history, and ethics. For the first time, Tarrants was forced to reexamine his beliefs—and he realized then how much he had been a slave to his ideology. His hunger for truth prompted him to reopen his Bible one summer night in 1970. At the time, asking God for forgiveness wasn't on his mind. Tarrants grew up in Alabama attending church every Sunday with his family. He had assumed he was saved. Even as he plotted terrorism, he had believed he was fighting for God and country. But reading Matthew 16:26 shook him awake: "For what will it profit a man if he gains the whole world and forfeits his soul? Or what shall a man give in return for his soul?" How utterly blind and foolish he had been to sell his soul in exchange for self-glory within the far-right movement! His hard heart cracked open, and he knelt on the concrete floor and asked Jesus Christ to forgive him.[1]

For those whom God begins to transform, the process is more than a change of worldviews; it involves living into a new identity. This Christian character is now able to bridge cultural differences and even love enemies. Tom Tarrants came to realize he could do more than overcome his hatred; he could come to love people of color. Through the help of advocates who believed his conversion was real, he was released from prison, eventually becoming a pastor and president of the C. S. Lewis Institute, all because Christ broke down his walls of hostility.

In the Sermon on the Mount, Jesus gives us a description of what God's coming kingdom will be like (Matt 5–7). It comes with an overwhelming sense of responsibility on our part. Jesus calls his followers to a new level of love and mercy. "You have heard what the law says . . . but I say to you even love your enemies" (Matt 5:43–44). Jesus expects much from us, but he also gives much of himself. After giving a picture of the kingdom in his Sermon on the Mount, Jesus then demonstrates the kingdom. Jesus teaches about love of enemies but then practices the love of outsiders. His teaching turns to touching the outcasts excluded in those days. In Matthew 8, Jesus reveals he is eager to help outsiders by breaking down the walls of religious, racial, and sexual boundaries. This wall breaker heals a leper, a gentile, and a woman, all outside the law and traditions of the times.[2] In the same way that Jesus healed Tom Tarrants to break down the walls of exclusion in his heart, Jesus healed these misfits to break down the walls that separated them from their community.

The leper was the archetype of what it meant to be an outsider, to be excluded. Lepers were considered to be under a curse and were commanded to cry "unclean, unclean" when coming near people. They were required to wear unkempt clothes and hair, while covering their lower lip, in order to be readily identified.

1. Lee, "Leaving Hate Behind."

2. Brunner, *Christ Book*. Many of the insights I share from Matthew 8 were gleaned from this commentary.

They were not allowed inside the walls of Jerusalem and for that reason were often seen begging for alms at the city gates. Even rabbis kept six feet away from these classic outsiders. All the more surprising when this leper "approached Jesus and knelt before him, saying, 'Lord, if you are willing you can heal me and make me clean'" (Matt 8:2). There is an inference from the leper that no one else had been willing to even come close, much less heal him. Jesus not only comes close, but before he says a word, "Jesus reached out and touched him" (Matt 8:3). He could have healed the man from six feet away with a spoken word, but instead Jesus provides a compassionate touch to this one who had been barred from all forms of religious and social life.

This willful touching of a leper breached the law and technically made Jesus unclean (Lev 5:3). But just as in the Sermon on the Mount, the Lord extends beyond the law to fulfill the law's intentions, in this case to bring wholeness in the form of a healing. Jesus's love and mercy enlarges the boundaries of our circle of comfort to include people our culture has dismissed or overlooked.

I watched my wife faithfully visit her mother in a nursing home. She suffered from Alzheimer's, and the last few years of her life, she didn't know her daughter. They would talk and together join in some of the numerous activities provided. Her mother especially liked to sing hymns. My wife would spend time with other residents who also could never remember that they had met just a few days earlier. There was very little ability to recognize or appreciate my wife's loving visits. There are times Jesus calls us to love people who cannot love us back; it may be because of mental or physical challenges, the shame of poverty, racial indifferences, or simply spiritual blindness. We may receive only small glimpses of appreciation. But just as Jesus loved us in the midst of our spiritual blindness and brokenness, so we continue to love those who are unable to reciprocate that love. There are many around us today who may be comparable to the lepers and outcasts of Jesus's day.

Who are the losers, the last, and the left behind in our culture today; the people we shun or shy away from because they cannot contribute to our well-being? Are they the mentally ill, the physically handicapped, the shut-ins, the non-white teenagers hanging out on our street corner, or maybe that noisy unemployed neighbor always looking to borrow something? Whoever makes our list of unfavorables, Christ will touch them first.

The next person Jesus encounters in Matthew's gospel is a centurion, a gentile, who begs him to come and heal his young servant. Only a leper was considered more unclean than a gentile, as Jews were forbidden to enter gentile homes. But even before this Roman officer can make a formal request to heal his servant, Jesus says, "I will come and heal him" (Matt 8:7). The significance of this is not only that the man was a gentile but also a Roman soldier. Jews were known to hate Romans and especially a Roman officer. No one challenges our prejudices and can provoke our hatred more than a member of a group we feel has unjustly treated our loved ones. Roman soldiers took religious oaths to serve the divine emperor. It is to this second representative, of all that is unclean and unworthy to Israel, that Jesus says, I want to come. Whatever refusals this man may have previously encountered, Jesus was eager to help.

Such willingness to assist people in need first requires an abandonment of all ethnic and racial prejudice. For it is not enough to simply respect people who are different than us; we must also love them. This is not always easy, as Philip Yancey writes:

> Diversity complicates rather than simplifies life. Perhaps for this reason we tend to surround ourselves with people of similar age, economic class, and opinion. Church offers a place where infants and grandparents, unemployed and executives, immigrants and blue bloods can come together. Just yesterday I sat sandwiched between an elderly man hooked up to a puffing oxygen tank and a breastfeeding baby who grunted loudly and contentedly throughout the sermon. When I walk into a new church, the more its members resemble each other—and resemble me—the more uncomfortable I feel.[3]

---

3. Yancey, "Denominational Diagnostics," 119.

The emergency waiting room is not unlike what the church can be, with a potential diversity unlike any other place in the world. I have had the opportunity of spending many hours waiting with parishioners for news concerning their family members. The room is filled with people who are different from one another. Yet they can't seem to do enough for each other. No one is rude. The distinctions of race and class melt away. A person is a parent first, and the color of the skin is second. The garbage man loves his wife as much as the corporate executive loves his, and everyone understands this. Each person pulls for everyone else. In this time and place, love reigns and the world changes. Positions and pretenses disappear. Everyone's focus is on the doctor's next report. If only it will show improvement! What is most important becomes common knowledge for everyone there.

This strange unity in diversity is further amplified in the cancer unit. No one is special. They all are battling a common enemy. Our son-in-law and assistant pastor discovered this in the final months before his death. He had a special gift for reaching over the fences people erected around their lives, but cancer had removed many of those barriers. His gift of listening and loving now went even deeper. In the strange and often painful world of cancer, differences fade in the light of authentic relationships, and real-life conversations take place. The statistics of status and the platitudes of politicians can no longer be heard, when the commonality of our humanity is embraced.

Jesus had touched a leper, the most despised and ostracized of all people in Israel, and healed him. Then he entered Capernaum and met the second most despised and offensive kind of person, a Roman centurion, and he healed him. Jesus is saying that with his coming kingdom, a radically new way of defining people is here. This was what Martin Luther King was pointing to in his most famous speech when he said, "I have a dream that my four little children will one day live in a nation where they will not be judged by the color of their skin but by the content of their character."[4] Jesus becomes the end of that ethnic and racial favoritism.

4. King, "I Have a Dream."

Jesus is not done breaking down the dividing walls of his culture. Jewish women were considered culturally half caste. They were limited to the Court of Women outside the temple and were regularly placed behind screens in the synagogues. Israelite men were known to offer prayers of thanks for not being born a women. Women were clearly seen as second-class citizens in the ancient and biblical worlds of Jesus. However, Jesus's unsolicited mercy touched Peter's mother-in-law, and her fever left her (Matt 8:15). No one, not even Peter, asks for her to be healed; she is not asked to believe or to pray for for her healing. There are no conditions required. God crosses this cultural divide, without being asked, in complete unmerited favor.

The leper, the gentile, and the woman are three pictures of God's generous grace. Three outsiders whose disdain God's grace will not recognize. Jesus created one new people on the cross, tearing down the dividing wall of hostility; now he has removed the walls of exclusion. Jesus the wall breaker heals outsiders and brings them in. He heals a leper, and down come the walls around the city; he heals the centurion's servant, and down come the walls of the Court of the Gentiles; he heals Peter's mother-in-law, and down come the walls of the Court of Women. The physically, racially, and sexually excluded are no longer outcasts. It's as if Matthew paints a portrait of Jesus walking up to the temple, breaking the barriers of exclusion; and on the cross, he will tear the curtain from top to bottom in the holy of holies, so all can come in. Blacks and whites, rich and poor, Protestants and Catholics, and, yes, even Democrats and Republicans can cross the lines that divide them and come together in unity.

In Northern Ireland, there's a city that's so divided, part of the population calls it Londonderry and the other part calls it Derry. In this city, Protestants live on the east bank and Catholics on the west bank. Many don't like to mix; so, one of the solutions was to build a bridge. The 900-foot bridge curves like a snake and is for walkers, joggers, and cyclists. They named it Peace Bridge. That's what they're trying to do, build a bridge, build peace, to be bridge builders in a world of walls. In our divided and often segregated society, we live among a body of humanity with a lot of different looking faces. Cultures, class, race, and our individual idiosyncrasies further separate us. We too must be bridge builders by overcoming our favoritism, our biases, and our prejudices, to bridge this world of walls and enter into the lives and cultures of others. This cannot happen from a distance, across town, or even from across the street. It certainly will not happen through politics, as God does not move on donkeys or elephants. It requires a walk across the bridge of differences and prejudices to engage in a time of listening and learning. It happens only when God's grace takes over.

There is a story about when Joshua was getting ready to go to war. He came across a giant of a man who was also getting ready to go into battle. He was a captain of a very large army. Joshua looked at him and asked, "Are you friend or foe?" Joshua needed to know whose side this man was on, because if he was with the opposition, then Joshua was going to lose. If he was on Joshua's side, then they could win. The man looked at him as if to say, you are obviously confused; I am neither on your side, nor am I on their side. "I am the commander of the Lord's army." I didn't come to take sides; I came to take over (Josh 5). Too often a political party, a denomination, a theological perspective, a race, or an ethnic group believes they have God, or a god, on their side in their respective war on culture. Scriptures such as the curse of Ham have been used to support slavery and to continue to subjugate people of color as inferior. At times, from television stations to church pulpits, Jesus is reformed into our own political or cultural likeness. As Tony Campolo once said, "God created us in his image, but we have decided to return the favor and create a God who is in our image."[5] I don't believe God has any interest in rebuilding the walls of our prejudices or the fences around our favorite group. Most of God's gracious work is about making us even before Christ's cross.

Jesus's parable in Matthew 20, about the vineyard workers, makes this point. Parables usually have one main object lesson to teach us. This parable instructs about the amazing grace of the

5. Campolo, as cited in Religious Herald, "Tony Campolo to Baptists."

God who continually lifts up the last, the least, and the latecomers. Those who are less effective, the least fruitful and the late bloomers, God raises up to a place of honor. Not because they have done great things, but because they have a great Lord. He is a Lord who invites some into the fields to work at the last possible hour and yet rewards them as if they had been there all day.

There are three things in this story we need to know about God's grace that makes us all even (Matt 20:1–10). First, the landowner goes out several times to find and hire workers for his vineyard. He hires one to start working at 6 a.m., one at 9 a.m., one at noon, and one at 3 p.m. We might call them the twelve-hour, the nine-hour, the six-hour, and the three-hour workers, respectively. Then at the eleventh hour, the landowner hires some latecoming help to work only one hour. All of this hiring was done at the initiative of the landowner. God is always the initiator of grace.

Second, God's grace is based on his promises. In the story, the landowner promises to pay a full day's wages to the twelve-hour worker, and to the others he promises to pay whatever is right, literally, what is righteous. Like the landowner, God fulfills his promises; we can count on it, his promises are guaranteed. Part of God's character is to do what he promises; he cannot lie. All the workers get paid a full day's wage.

This brings us to the third and final lesson to be learned. The promise was to pay a full day's wage to the twelve-hour worker and whatever was fair to the other workers. But what is fair? Was it fair to pay all the workers the same as the one who had worked all day, especially the one who had worked only one hour? "You've paid them just as much as you paid us who worked all day in the scorching heat" (Matt 20:12). The complaint is not that the landowner broke his promise or cheated or was unrighteous. The problem in their eyes was that he gave the same pay to the undeserving. The real complaint was that he made them all equal. God's grace makes us all even. To some that is unfair, even scandalous; to others it is extravagant, an amazing grace. The response from the landowner, and subsequently from God, comes in the form of two questions. Don't I have the right to do what I want with my money, and are you jealous because I was kind to others? (Matt 20:15). The first question relates to God's sovereignty and the second to man's pride. The complaint questions who is in charge and whether one really needs the grace of God. I want to decide what I deserve and whether others are worthy to receive the same as me. The last become first through grace, and the first become last through pride.

This parable not only teaches that God's grace makes us even but is a warning to those who would look down on others. It warned the Pharisees to not look down on the Jewish Christians, it warned the Jewish Christians not to look down on the gentiles, and it warned Catholics not to look down on the latecoming Protestants. It warns all who would see themselves as superior based on race, politics, or economics. Jesus's healing of the leper, the gentile, and the woman make the same point as Jesuss' parable about paying all the vineyard workers the same wage. His priority is always for the outcast, the excluded, and the last.

Jesus the wall breaker challenges the prejudices we carry in our hearts, hidden away and covered up. Racism, classism, sexism—all the -isms that insist on a level of superiority based on status, gender, skin color, or our own righteousness—reveal those prejudices. Anything in our hearts that sends someone outside the walls of our Jerusalem exposes our bias and bigotry. When we believe we live exclusively in the holy of holies, there will always be someone or some group whom we feel doesn't measure up.

Chapter 4

Peter's Journey to Overcome Favoritism

I THINK MOST PEOPLE agree that prejudice and racism are a problem today. However, the temptation is to think it's not a problem with me. We can find at least one example that we think disqualifies us from having prejudices or a racial bias. We have a Black worship leader at church, my co-worker is Black, or my new neighbor is Hispanic. This can't be a problem with me. I am not the one discriminating or treating others as inferior based on their skin color. Yet most white people live and worship with their dominant culture, rarely engaging across racial, ethnic, or socio-political divisions.

The word prejudice is a shortened word for prejudging someone without all the evidence. Some have said it is a great shortcut to form an opinion without spending the time to get all the facts. We assume certain things about people by the car they drive, the clothes they wear, or the tattoos adorning their bodies. We may avoid conversations at social gatherings based on a person's profession. Is the person a lawyer or a store clerk?

Racism takes on a new level when you add power to the word prejudice. When our prejudice has the ability to adversely affect the life of another person, either individually or institutionally, then racism is in play. It happens when people are overlooked for a promotion, underpaid, or uninvited, based on their ethnicity or race. I have accompanied African Americans when they went to look at an apartment owned by a white landlord. I had experienced too many situations where they were told the apartment had already been rented, only to see it was still available days later. Right or wrong, a white pastor could sometimes bring out a more truthful reception.

Unfortunately, racism and prejudices are a universal problem. It is not just an American problem; it is a human problem. It is a problem of the heart called sin, and sin distorts the way we see ourselves, others, and God. It is like those mirrors at festivals that distort the way our body and face look. Racism and prejudice are spiritual problems that affect the way we see others as different than us, and they cannot be fixed with legislation or a seminar. They can be overcome only by understanding the image of God *in* us and what Christ accomplished on the cross *for* us.

The full title of Charles Darwin's work in 1859 was *The Origin of Species by Means of Natural Selection, or the Preservation of Favored Races in the Struggle for Life*. However you may view Darwin's theory of evolution, it increased the thinking about favored races. Racism was common before 1859, but the acceptance of evolutionary theory only enhanced the biological arguments for it, suggesting that some races were more advanced than others.

In Acts 17:26, the author writes, "From one blood he created all the nations throughout the whole earth." We were not only all created, but we are all related. We can trace our ancestry to the same human family. We must acknowledge this shared humanity and that we all have the image of God in us.

I never understood why certain clothes could be so expensive. How can a shirt at one store cost hundreds of dollars and a similar shirt cost under forty dollars at a different store? I have learned it is all about the designer. One shirt is more valuable because of who the designer is, especially if his or her name is on the shirt. The value is not determined by the color or size; its value is dictated by who designed it. Our value and significance has nothing to do with the color of our skin but everything to do with the author of life.

God has stamped his signature on each one of us while at the same time creating no two people who are exactly the same. We all have the same inherent value regardless of our race, gender, appearance, or age, because we have been designed and created by the God of the universe.

So why are we afflicted with favoritism, prejudices, and racism? Because sin distorts how we see each other. We need a new mirror or a new lens to view the image of God in others. This is where Christ's work on the cross comes in, where the walls of hostility between racial and ethnic groups were broken down. The cross of Christ convicts us that our sin does not see the image of God in one another; our sight is warped. When we accept what Christ has done, we realize there is no place for superiority nor prejudice. We repent, we ask for forgiveness, and we start a process of seeing others from God's point of view.

Peter began such a process. Peter had received a vision of food that he and other Jews were forbidden to consume, but God told Peter to go ahead and eat. Peter declined in an effort to uphold the dietary laws of never eating anything impure and unclean. But a voice spoke again, saying, "Do not call something unclean if God has made it clean" (Acts 10:15). Peter was confused as to what this all could mean. While puzzling over this vision, he was informed that men had come to take him to the house of Cornelius, a Roman officer. On his arrival, the entire household was waiting for him, and it was explained that they had been instructed to send for a man named Simon Peter to hear the message of God. It became clear to Peter that God had given him a vision of food in order to apply it to persons, specifically to the unclean gentiles. Peter, now inside a gentile household and breaking Jewish law, declares, "I see very clearly that God shows no favoritism" (Acts 10:34). However, Peter's revelation is an action in process. His statement in the Greek is in the present tense, which means it has ongoing implications. Peter was saying, I have just begun, for the first time, to recognize for myself that God is not partial. He may have known it intellectually, but the full understanding had not previously registered with him until then. This is the reality for dealing with our own favoritism and prejudices; overcoming them is a process. Our brains prefer the path of least resistance, and in our sinful nature, prejudices remain hidden. It would take ten more years for Peter to fully recognize this.

For years, Peter was hanging out on the other side of the tracks, with his gentile friends, eating barbecued pork and singing his favorite gospel songs. This cross-cultural experience was having a great impact on him. Then some of his Jewish homeboys showed up to tell Peter this is not the way you were brought up, you don't belong on this side of town. "He was afraid of criticism from these people who insisted on the necessity of circumcision" (Gal 2:12). Peter stopped eating with the gentiles, and others followed his hypocrisy, including Barnabas the great encourager. The thing is, Barnabas was raised a gentile, born and schooled in Cypress. Yet, he too followed Peter, withdrawing from gentile fellowship because of the pressure. The potency of prejudices can cause even a good man to embrace prejudicial attitudes and actions.

It is in times like this that members of the majority culture need to speak up and confront the sin of racism. Paul, a Jewish leader, opposed Peter to his face, saying "what he did was very wrong . . . by not following the truth of the gospel" (Gal 2:11, 14). Peter and the circumcision party were out of step with the gospel; they were no longer following Christ on this issue. Paul confronted this hypocrisy, this inconsistent Christianity, and not just to Peter's face but in front of all those gathered in Antioch.

One of the biggest setbacks for overcoming our prejudices is when the prevailing culture wants the non-whites among them to assimilate, to accept their traditions and viewpoints, in order to be fully accepted. Jews wanted gentiles to follow the ceremonial laws of their heritage. Both groups were under God's moral laws, but with Jesus's coming and his work on the cross, the ceremonial laws had been fulfilled. Some today believe you must have a particular political view to be considered a true Christian, or the right mode of baptism, or the proper attire for church. Scripture is clear that God accepts us sinners by his grace though faith in the finished work of Christ. Who are we to withhold fellowship or withdraw from anyone whom God has justified?

I usually did not address politics from the pulpit, but on the Sunday after Barack Obama's first election I simply noted the historic nature of this event, especially for the half of our congregation who were African Americans. The next morning I received a scathing email for commending this man's election, considering his view on abortion. This was from a young couple whom I had counseled and married a few years earlier. I talked by phone with the husband, I listened patiently, and then I invited him to meet with me and the three African American elders from our church. I wanted him to hear our elders' perspective based on their experience as Blacks. We began by assuring him that our church was holistically pro-life, something he already knew. The conversation was gracious, but it became apparent there were underlying prejudices that were being exposed by the election of our first Black president. He and his wife ultimately could not see past their issue and never returned to the church. Their decision was not in step with the gospel, but as difficult as it was for everyone involved, we had peace that we had gently and lovingly opposed their hypocrisy.

Hypocrisy literally means playacting. Hypocrites were actors on a stage who would hold various masks over their face representing the character they were playing. Peter was a Christian, but his actions towards the gentiles revealed a character different than a Christ follower. His withdrawal from the gentiles was not based on any biblical principle but rather on his fear of his Jewish culture. It is not enough to believe the gospel; we must also practice it. Paul made it clear that Peter's requirements for the gentiles to keep the law "treats the grace of God as meaningless" (Gal 2:21).

What might have happened if Paul had not confronted Peter and those not following the gospel truth? Would a permanent Jewish and gentile split have occurred? Or would this new Jewish sect, called the Way, have stagnated? Paul knew the truth, and effectiveness of the gospel was at stake. The question is, how much is the segregated church today contradicting the gospel? How well is the church preserving and applying the gospel, including its witness to our secular unbelieving world? How can we expect our culture to overcome its divisions of race and politics when we show favoritism and our racial bias is on display?

Dr. Martin Luther King Jr. delivered a sermon in November of 1954 titled "Transformed Nonconformist." Here is part of what he preached: "The Christian is called upon not to be like a thermometer conforming to the temperature of his society but he must be like a thermostat serving to transform the temperature of his society . . . . I have seen many white people who sincerely oppose segregation and discrimination but they never took a real stand against it because of fear of standing alone."[1] Peter evidently feared standing alone against those insisting the gentiles must be circumcised to be included in the Christian faith. As Dr. King implies, it is easier to intellectually oppose racism and racial bias but another thing to act against such things. Soren Kierkegaard writes, "The admirer is infatuated with the false security of greatness; but if there is any inconvenience or trouble, he pulls back. . . . Christ never asks for admirers, worshipers, or adherents. No, he calls disciples."[2]

Nonconformity should not be pursued just for the sake of being different or to gain attention. This is why Paul instructs us to not only resist conforming to the world but also to "be transformed by the renewal of your mind" (Rom 12:2). We need this new mental outlook to discern right and wrong instead of relying on popular polls or the consensus of the crowds. The popular thought of people about the kingdom was that the Messiah would come to establish a new political power to overthrow the Roman Empire. When Jesus made it clear to his disciples that he must go to Jerusalem, suffer many things, and be killed and resurrected, Peter sided with the majority view, saying, "This should not happen to you." Jesus response to Peter was a quick rebuff, "Get away from me, Satan! You are seeing things merely from a human point of view, not from God's" (Matt 16:22–23). Peter was conforming to the majority opinion, but Jesus was not going to succumb to

1. King, "Transformed Nonconformist."
2. Kierkegaard, "Followers, Not Admirers," 55.

the pressure of the crowd. He had orders from God his Father to establish a new kind of kingdom. Martin Lindstrom, a former market researcher and author of *Branwashed*, argues: "There is ample research to show that we instinctively look to the behaviors of others to inform the decisions we make—everything from which way we should walk, to what music we should listen to, to which kind of car we should drive. It seems, in short, that we instinctively believe that others know more about what we want than we ourselves do."[3]

Psychologists have a name for this phenomenon. It's called peer pressure. We all know football referees are unbiased, right? They would never be influenced by fans or football players. Well, according to a recent study, football refs are often swayed by their surroundings. Michael Lopez, a researcher and statistician at Skidmore College in New York, led a study that found referees are much more likely to make calls that favor the team whose coaches and players are on the sideline closer to the potential penalty. Lopez analyzed five years of NFL games, including 1,400 penalty calls where the action happened close to one team's sideline or the other. One of the files he examined was whether referees called a late hit on a player. If one player is tackling another, he's allowed to do it while the opposing player is within bounds but not if he's out of bounds. But the bodies are usually flying into one another near a sideline. It's what's called a bang-bang play: it all happens so quickly, and the refs have to make a judgment call. Lopez measured how often these kinds of judgment calls go in favor of the team whose coaches are on the sideline closest to where the potential penalty is taking place. He found referees are much more likely to make calls that comply with what people nearest to them are demanding. In short, intimidation works. Pressure the refs, get in their face, and they will often cave into social pressure.[4]

This kind of pressure crosses over into our racial attitudes and behaviors as well. "Theories of modern or symbolic racism hold that prejudicial attitudes are learned from influential role models

3. Lindstrom, *Brandwashed,* 104–8.
4. Inskeep, host, "Study: NFL Referees Influenced."

and society more generally."[5] This reality, coupled with our brains' preference to seek the path of least resistance, helps us understand Peter's about-face. We too are susceptible to the peer pressure of role models and the culture of social media when it comes to racial issues. We may think we are intellectually showing no partiality when it comes to race and economics, but as Martin Luther King suggested, we might not take a stand against racism or discrimination for fear of standing out from the prevailing crowd.

These past few years, with the tension between Blacks and the police over the shootings that took place, many in the white community felt sorrow but few shared any verbal outrage with the underlying racial bias. There was the lingering question whether the shootings were justified, and with the heightened rhetoric, most white people were afraid to speak out. Fear of conflict and standing alone often ruled the day.

In the neighborhoods where I lived and pastored for nearly four decades, if I observed a young hooded black man with a cell phone exchange something through a car window, there is what I call a sensible probability that a drug deal just went down. I could be wrong but . . . However, if I then form a judgment that all hooded black men with cell phones are drug dealers, I have crossed a line into a sinful prejudice. That line is not always clear, but nevertheless it is a real line, and God sees it even if I don't.

It's that same sinful prejudice that keeps much of the white church and community silent when another innocent black man is gunned down by two white men whose prejudice further crossed that line onto an act of murder. It's our sinful prejudice that wants to believe that racism doesn't exist and there must be some reasonable explanation for this horrible incident and others like it. The thing about a sinful prejudice is that it keeps the truth hidden in the dark closets of our mind and keeps our tongues tied from protesting the injustice.

While it is true we will never be able to fully comprehend or feel the racial prejudice our Black brothers and sisters have experienced, it should not keep us from crying out with them and

5. Kinder and Sanders, *Divided by Color*, 291.

standing against this continued racial injustice. It's time for the majority culture and the church to repent from its silence, to speak up and ask the Black community how we can help.

Like Peter, it may take a number of years to overcome our inherent prejudices and favoritisms, but it is time to start the process, it is time to fully walk in step with the gospel. Years after Peter was confronted by Paul, Peter wrote in his first epistle, "Remember that the heavenly Father to whom you pray has no favorites" (1 Pet 1:17). We trust that Peter had continued his journey of overcoming favoritism.

Chapter 5

Tearing Down the Fences
to Neighbor Loving

WHEN WE STUDY THE stories of Jesus, his teaching and his viewpoint are everything. It is like when a young baby first looks into a mirror. When the baby moves, the reflection moves; when the baby waves, the reflection waves; and then suddenly as the baby's face lights up, there is the realization that it's itself. That is what can happen to us when we read Jesus's parables. We are reading the black-and-white print and all of a sudden we see a reflection of ourselves in the story. I think this is often the case in the parable of the good Samaritan (Luke 10:25–37).

A young lawyer, a theologian, wants to question Jesus. He is not really sincere about his inquiry. What he wants is to build his reputation as a scholar at the expense of what he perceives is a dull Galilean peasant. He wants to prove his intellect in a courtroom-like argument. He has prepared the whole conversation like a legal brief. He knows how he will start, how he thinks Jesus will answer, and how he will respond. Like a courtroom joust, it won't take long before he has Jesus cornered. The young lawyer begins with the question of the ages: "Teacher, what should I do to inherit eternal life?" Jesus countered with a question of his own: "What is the greatest commandment?" Anyone who grew up around the people of God knew the answer to that question, so he proudly replied, "You shall love the Lord your God with all of your heart, soul, strength, and mind, and your neighbor as yourself." Jesus said, "Right. Do this and you will live" (Luke 10:28). Everyone considered him a religious man, so the first part of the answer was not a problem, but he wasn't sure about the neighbor thing. Feeling a little trapped and attempting to justify himself, the lawyer asked, "Who is my neighbor?" He wanted to define the word neighbor. I think we can empathize with that. How many times have we read a clear requirement of Scripture, but we are not sure we want to follow it? We begin debating it in our mind and asking friends for their opinion. Maybe we can find a justification or an exception to let us off the hook. We attempt to reshape God's word to fit into our lives rather than letting our lives be formed by Scripture. Author and professor Dr. Haddon Robinson states: "A kind of arithmetic has been spawned in the counting rooms of hell. This kind of arithmetic is always interested in reaching the masses but somehow never gets down to a man or a woman. This kind of arithmetic always talks about winning the world for God but doesn't think about winning a neighborhood for God. That arithmetic makes it valiant to cross oceans but never really crosses streets."[1]

This is the arithmetic the expert in religious law wants to use. He wants to keep his discussion about loving neighbors in a general and philosophical realm. Let's talk about the *idea* of loving my neighbor. In general, what kind of people *are* my neighbors? The American poet Carl Sandburg once wrote, "Love your neighbor as yourself; but don't take down the fence."[2] That is what Luke's Gospel tells us this religious expert wanted to do. He knew that loving neighbors was connected to inheriting eternal life, but he wanted to limit his responsibility to his kind of folk. In other words, he was hoping there were some people who were not his neighbors. He had answered the question correctly about what the law required, but faced with having to act on it, he asks, "Who is my neighbor?" This religious lawyer wants to know the answer to that question in

1. Robinson, "Case Study of Mugging."
2. Sandburg, *People, Yes*, 107.

general terms, but Jesus answers with the question if you're willing to be a neighbor in specific terms. The lawyer is focused on the people group to be loved, and Jesus focuses on the love for a specific person. In Scripture, Christian love does not reside in the personality being loved but in the person doing the loving. In other words, we are not called to love our neighbor because they are lovable but because it reflects our love for God.

A careful study of the Hebrew word for love in Leviticus 19:18 (the Scripture quoted by the lawyer) reveals that it is a love that is useful or beneficial to your neighbor. We are to be beneficial or helpful to our neighbors as ourselves. This alters the self-centered idea that we must love ourselves before we can love our neighbor.

Jesus drives his point home by telling the story of a man beaten, robbed, disrobed, and left for dead. Since his clothes have been removed, we don't know the socio-economic status of the man, just that he lies there naked and left for dead. Then by chance help appears, not once but twice. First a Jewish priest and then a temple assistant, a Levite. They look, they assess the situation, and then they walk away. No reason is given as to why they refuse to help, but we all know getting involved is usually risky and costly. It is also a moral failure.

In his mind, the priest may have had legitimate religious reasons. In the Old Testament, a priest could become ceremoniously unclean if he touched a dead body. He would not want to go through all the time and expense of the cleansing rituals. And possibly all the many questions about what he was being cleansed from would not be good for his reputation. There are places we could go and activities we could engage in that might harm our good name. We desire people to hold us in high regard, and so we too may cross to the other side of the road to avoid the person in need. While the Levite probably did not have defilement as a concern, he may have simply been in a hurry to get to Jerusalem to teach a biblical lesson. We don't know for sure what these men were thinking and why they did not stop to help. I do know most of us have done something similar. The fences of the time required and our preferred activities with our favorite people keep us from crossing the road to be a good neighbor.

Then another traveler comes by. A despised Samaritan, a half-breed, who completely turns the cultural expectations upside down by becoming the model neighbor and the perfect example of selfless concern. He bandages the man's wounds, he takes him to an inn and pays for his care. His mercy was inconvenient and costly, for which he received no reward or recognition. The bad guy becomes the good guy in Jesus's story. When Jesus asks the expert in religious law, "Now which of these three would you say was a neighbor to the man who was attacked by bandits?," the lawyer can't even mention the man's race. He simply says, "The one who showed him mercy" (Luke 10:36–37). He remains choosy about his neighbors.

Most of us think of neighbors as those for whom we do something. They are the ones to whom we lend our tools or the ones we invite to church. They are usually the ones who belong in our neighborhood, whom we help out when they have a need and we have the time. But Jesus did not say the neighbor was the one left half dead beside the road. The neighbor was the Samaritan. Being a neighbor, according to Jesus, often requires risk and sacrifice to come alongside people in need who may not be a part of our group. From Jesus's viewpoint, "being good in the traditional, legalistic sense was not at all the same thing as loving God or loving one's neighbor."[3]

In Jesus's parable, the priest and the Levite were more than just individuals. They also represented a social structure at the time. Priests had the structural role of protecting and preserving the Jewish culture. The Levites assisted the priests in the temple but were also members of the permanent Sanhedrin, giving them a major responsibility in the administration of justice.[4] Representing those respective social systems, the structures themselves failed to meet the need of the man robbed and left for dead. Today our secular and political structures have replaced many of those

3. Hoyer and McDaniel, "From Jericho to Jerusalem," 329.
4. Smith, *Smith's Bible Dictionary*, 347.

roles, partially because the church has neglected its responsibilities in caring for the least of these. Although the truth is, neither the church nor any of our systems is being a very good neighbor to those who have been beaten down on the road of life.

America's southern border continues to be enveloped in a humanitarian crisis, as refugees fleeing violence in central America seek safety. It's a complex issue, because border security is a legitimate need. Yet innocent children and families are escaping violent drug wars exploding all around them. It's the illogical immigration system that further incites the problem, empowering the cartels and the traffickers. Immigration reform isn't about making immigration easier. It's about making the system consistent and sensible, so that we know who is here lawfully and who isn't. The good Samaritan story doesn't give the details on how to create a just system to balance both border security and respect for human life. But the gospel does tell us that our instinct ought to be one of compassion toward those in need, not disgust or anger.

However, before we dismiss our personal responsibility with the failure of our immigration and social systems, we need to be reminded that individuals create these broken structures. From the *Journal of Psychology and Theology*, Stephen Hoyer and Patrice McDaniel share: "Even though Jesus was telling a story, he was still talking about reality. Psychological research tells us that strange as it may seem people really do act in the ways he described. Knowing this, Jesus presented his story in such a way that people could find themselves in the story and thus make the story their own."[5]

A true neighbor overcomes the social structures and takes down the individual racial fences that divide. Doing so can not only encourage others to do the same but may initiate systemic change. Matt Perman, referencing Tim Keller's book *Generous Justice*, asks readers to consider a sequel to this parable. Imagine the Samaritan starts traveling the road again and comes across another person left for dead on the side of the road. A few weeks later, this happens again. Soon, every time he makes the trip to Jericho, he

5. Hoyer and McDaniel, "From Jericho to Jerusalem," 332.

comes across people lying in the road. Hundreds of people are now ending up along the road, beaten and robbed. What should this Samaritan do? This is the question of social justice. When we see multiple people in need, we of course still give whatever personal help we can, but if we are truly to love our neighbor as ourselves, we also need to give thought to how we can address the underlying conditions that are causing so many people to fall into that situation in the first place.[6]

Children, the homeless, ex-prisoners, the mentally ill, the unemployed, single mothers, immigrants, the sexually broken and those who are racially different are being overlooked and abandoned. Much of the church and society cross to the other side of the street, to mind our own business. Too often, if others don't have something we want or can't contribute to what we need, we build a fence to keep a safe distance. And it isn't just those who are considered weak and wounded whom we are tempted to exclude and abandon. A Hollywood hedonism that puts pleasure over pain, a Wall Street materialism that puts prosperity over poverty, a cultural individualism that puts privacy over people, and a church pragmatism that puts function over faith leave us capable of walking past just about anybody who is not in our group.

What is needed are neighbors and neighbor churches who will cross the street of ethnic and economic discrimination, who will take the risk and pay the cost when systems and structures fail to act as neighbors. We are talking about people who will see every person in a neighborhood as someone created in God's image and churches concerned with a community's needs and interests. These are actions that allow the stranger, whether there is an obvious need or not, to be one with us in church and in our lives. My experience tells me people respond best not when they are given choices but when they are chosen and invited to become a friend or a member of a community. The fences we erect limit our encounters with disparate people who have the potential to help us to grow.

---

6. Keller, *Generous Justice*, as cited in Perman, "Business."

God called Abraham to leave his home to become a blessing to the nations, to people he did not know. In order to be such a blessing to strangers, he had to become a vulnerable stranger himself. His entire story is one of the struggle between self-preservation and living out his calling as a homeless sojourner. Author Parker Palmer writes: "The need to feel at home turns out to be idolatry, because it involves finding our security in position and place rather than in dependence on God. If we live in God we will find ourselves on pilgrimage; we will be taken to alien places where we are strangers and estranged. Only when we acknowledge that we can't go home again, will we be on the road to faith."[7]

With literal fences in our lives and protective guards around our hearts, we create comfortable spaces where well-intended activity happens but little blessing to the stranger takes place. We often forget or lack an understanding of what it is like to be a stranger, to be on the outside looking in—although I think most of us could recall even some minimal experience, as an adult or from childhood, where we were left out or excluded. At a very young age, I was not allowed to play hockey with my friends because the ice rink attendant thought I was too small. At a denominational committee meeting to choose our key note speaker for our annual assembly, I asked if we had ever considered inviting one of our small church pastors to speak. The uncomfortable silence was finally broken by a call to once again nominate a speaker from one of our esteemed megachurches. Being excluded for your size, as a person or a church, is a far cry from racial discrimination, but it was enough to remind me of what it is like to be an outsider.

Moses tells Israel that they were not to oppress foreigners or strangers because they knew the heart of a stranger (Exod 23:9). Their experience as foreigners in the land of Egypt should motivate them to bless the stranger among them. The Hebrew word for heart should be understood as "the deeply personal knowledge derived from close involvement with the other person."[8] The

7. Palmer, *Company of Strangers*, 63.
8. Hanson, *People Called*, 46.

Israelites had a deeply heartfelt experience of being strangers in Egypt, and we might do well to recall at least one incident where we felt out of place. The disadvantage most of us have, of not really knowing the heart of a stranger, is we have a dominant group to which we can retreat behind the fence. Even living and worshipping among the African American culture in the inner city, if we ever felt unaccepted, we could resort to the safety net of a white middle-class lifestyle.

Being a neighbor, as Jesus describes it in the story of the good Samaritan, is an intentional act of love. It means tearing down the fences we have erected as barriers to love across our differences. How can we do that when we have nothing in common or, even worse, hate the person on the other side of the cultural divide? Colossians 3:14 says, "Above all, clothe yourselves with love, which binds us all together in perfect harmony." Paul uses the metaphor of clothing ourselves, like putting on a coat of love resulting in a belt of harmony that wraps around everything else. The word for love here has an element of kindness and helpfulness to all people, with no interest or expectation for receiving anything in return. Imagine what that might look like for the irritating family next door or the activist on the other side of your political aisle, or the person of color in the neighborhood whom you have stereotyped as unfriendly. Invite them over for coffee, take some baked goods to their home, ask how you might pray for them, and above all, when you get the opportunity, listen to their story. Listening is the real challenge in this initial attempt to tear down the cultural fence. The distracting voices of our heritage and the pragmatic counsel of our own race will drown out Jesus's words of racial and ethnic unity. In the prophet Ezekiel's words, "They have ears but refuse to hear. For they are a rebellious people" (Ezek 12:2).

When it comes to listening it is worth revisiting Volf's double vision. We must realize that we will rarely understand the person across the cultural aisle from our objective standpoint. We must take a step outside ourselves to examine the truths we hold about others different than us. This requires a willingness, as Volf writes, "to entertain the idea that these 'verities' may be but so many ugly prejudices, bitter fruits of our imaginary fears, or our sinister desires to dominate or exclude."[9] After that uncomfortable exercise of self-discovery, we then listen carefully to how the other person views her- or himself and how she or he sees us. We then attempt to imagine "why their perspective about themselves, about us . . . can be so plausible to them whereas it is implausible . . . even offensive to us."[10] Finally we invite the other into the universe of our life to reflect about what we are learning about each other. While perspectives may change, that is not the necessary goal at this early stage of the process. The goal is to keep the relationship moving forward and to gain some common language and common understanding of each other's perspective. The challenge of this ongoing process is not just the struggle but the lack of any immediate fruit. We are usually willing to suffer a little if it will bring about a desired result or at least some sense of appreciation from God and others. Yet, Volf says this was the great scandal of the cross, as both God and the disciples abandoned Jesus. We cannot claim the benefits of the cross without a willingness to embrace those who suffer discrimination and prejudices, as well as the setbacks and rejections that may come with the journey.

The hope we have in this work of dismantling the fences of separation is not in the visible results of changed perspectives or the hope of fixing our world with social control or rational thought. Our greater hope is in the future joy of a resurrected life and reconciled relationships.

---

9. Volf, *Exclusion and Embrace*, 251.

10. Volf, *Exclusion and Embrace*, 252.

Chapter 6

Bridging Cultural Divisions

THERE IS A CHINESE proverb that says, "If you want to know what water is, don't ask a fish." A fish doesn't understand its own environment until it enters dry land and struggles to survive. In a similar way, no one culture can know itself fully until it enters into the cultural environment of another. As we bridge the cultural divide to embrace those different than us, we come to a greater appreciation of our own culture, but more importantly, we become aware of our cultural idols.

There is no such thing as a culture-free expression of the Christian faith; all of Christianity has been distorted by cultural prejudices. As mentioned earlier, the Enlightenment has partially blinded American Christianity to the spirit world, while some Africans' heritage of superstition has distorted their view of this non-physical part of life. Who is right? Both worldviews have been affected by their culture. Some cultures put a very high value on getting an appropriate return on their investment of time, talent, and treasure, while others focus more on relationships at the expense of time.

Only when we allow the relationship with someone from a different heritage to honestly critique our cultural expressions of faith can we see our prejudices. We need our brothers and sisters from across the cultural divide to help us identify potential idols.

Especially for us Eurocentric Christians, the danger is to put our cultural identity above our Christian beliefs without even knowing it. Accountability and love with others across racial and ethnic divisions helps us to better critique and complete our own faith traditions, whether that is our individual faith, our neighbors, our church, or our denomination.

In the first few years of our interracial church, we began a Wednesday night gathering called Fudge Ripple Night, a name we borrowed from a church in Chicago. We came together to begin to get to know one another across our racial differences over ice cream. At first our discussions were limited to food, clothes, hair styles, and other stereotypes of culture. While seemingly insignificant, we learned not all Black folks liked chitlins, and some of the white women wanted to know how to make their counterparts' mac'n'cheese. However, we knew relationships were progressing when the Blacks in the group felt safe enough to insist that we needed to add chocolate marshmallow to our weekly menu for a more equal representation. This fellowship laid a foundation of trust for accountability and critique of each other's cultures and customs.

We live in a clash of cultures: political, class, racial, and religious. In over forty years of life and ministry in the inner city, I found myself teaching how so many well-meaning Christians would unknowingly apply the term ROI, "return on investment," to their efforts in our ministry. If they were going to invest in a person or a program, they expected a proper return on their time or energy spent. An improvement on a report card, the appropriate thankful attitude, or a change in some addictive behavior—some measurement of success was expected for their gracious efforts. The law of achievement was being applied to a people ruled by poverty and violence, whose skin was often considered the wrong color to succeed and who had little hope that any of this would change. It contradicted the very nature of the gospel. It asked people to justify the help they received with some measure of achievement, and if they failed, it continued to shatter their dignity and envelop them in despair. However, the gospel taught them that they were not defined by these outside influences of the law, a gospel we attempted to not only proclaim but to embody in our church and community.

Like a fish is clueless about water, Anglo-Americans are culturally unaware of their environment. We live our public and private lives in the same privileged culture, blinded by our affinity for consumerism and individualism. Consequently, our cultural intelligence and competence is limited. Eric Law, in his book *The Wolf Shall Dwell with the Lamb,* writes that there are two parts to culture: "External culture is the conscious part of culture. It is the part that we can see, taste and hear. It consists of acknowledged beliefs and values. It is explicitly learned and can be easily changed. However, this constitutes only a small part of our culture. The major part is the internal part, which consists of the unconscious beliefs, through patterns, values and myths that affect everything we do and see. It is implicitly learned and it is very hard to change."[1] It is this internal part of culture that makes it so difficult for our majority population to overcome its unconscious beliefs and myths about race and class.

This cultural blind spot is often applied to our reading of Scripture, ignoring some parts and embellishing other parts, based on our sociocultural position or political view. D. A. Carson calls this reductionism "taming Scripture by not letting all of it speak to us."[2] Richard Lints, in his book *The Fabric of Theology,* seeks to avoid a potential spectrum of reductionist extremes: a cultural fundamentalism where the Bible is seen as culture free and a cultural relativism where one believes culture gives meaning to the Bible.[3] Both spectrums are used to justify a one-way cultural bridge. The truth is, the Bible will offend and support many aspects of a given culture. For example, Scripture has much to say about wealth and poverty. It affirms the right to private property, while at the same time, it teaches personal responsibility to care for the poor.

1. Law, *Wolf Shall Dwell with Lamb,* 5.
2. Carson, *Biblical Interpretation and Church,* 23.
3. Lints, *Fabric of Theology,* 101–3.

In Galatians 6:1–5, Paul writes about someone who has been overtaken by sin. We don't know if the sin was personal or a systemic injustice, but sin was the one in pursuit. The result is a burden has come into this person's life and he or she needs help. It is like a boulder that has caused a disruption in life that is simply too heavy for one to overcome. Paul instructs us to share those burdens and thus fulfill the law of Christ, that is to fulfill the requirement to love our neighbors (Gal 6:2). This burden lifting is to be done in humility and gentleness, not overestimating our own importance. The temptation is for the helpers to think of themselves as superior, especially if there is an underlying racial or class bias. Sharing the removal of a paralyzing circumstance in a person's life can be time consuming and costly. Walking alongside one is rarely a brief one-time event, as it often requires helping the person with a change in personal habits or the challenges of addressing any systemic issues. Either way, the goal is to help people to be "responsible for their own load" (Gal 6:5). In the Greek, the word "load" is a different word from the word "burden" in verse 2. We can think of load as a divine knapsack sewn on our backs—God-given responsibilities. Paul had instructed the church that those who were capable yet unwilling to work should not get to eat (2 Thess 3:10). Parents have a responsibility to their children, and children are responsible to honor their parents. Not everyone will respond appropriately to this burden-sharing help. Sometimes the burden becomes a way of life, and there is no timetable that comes with the instructions for sharing each other's burdens. We persevere, we serve, we befriend, and we love, while being wise as serpents and gentle as doves. I don't give addicts twenty dollars cash, but I will go with them and buy a meal, take them to rehab, and listen to their story. How often and how long should one help? I can't answer that. Sooner or later though, we will need to ask the question Jesus asked the cripple at the pool at Bethesda, "Would you like to get well?" (John 5:6).

We can see in this biblical story an example of how Scripture can both challenge and encourage different views concerning wealth and poverty. Those in plenty, who may have a more capitalistic outlook, are called to assist those in want, perhaps a socialist's view of things. Yet those in need are not to make their desperate circumstances a lifestyle but instead become responsible and productive members of their community. We can see in the wisdom of Proverbs that a lack of personal responsibility can result in poverty (Prov 10:4), but at the same time Proverbs 13:23 says, "A poor man's farm may produce much food but injustice sweeps it all away." The Bible denounces both irresponsibility and systems in favor of the rich. This becomes the common ground for diverging cultural views of economics and politics. Finding common ground is the key for bridging all our cultural divisions. Common ground helps one cultural view, whether socioeconomic, political, or racial, from acting or even feeling superior. Whether we are in the racial majority, are wealthy, or claim a social status, each one must recognize all we have is by the grace of God. This is not easy for many of us. Pride in our hard work and efforts can keep us from realizing the extent of God's gracious hand in our lives and subsequently hinder our response to cultural differences.

Paul requires us to refrain from trying to impress others, and he counted everything he owned as garbage compared to his knowledge of Christ (Phil 2:3, 3:8). This humility enabled him to be "with those who are weak and share their weakness . . . to find common ground with everyone" (1 Cor 9:22). The apostle was willing to limit his freedom for the sake of the gospel, to welcome, listen, and be compassionate to others unlike him. This was not easy, as he had to discipline himself like an athlete in training.

With years of life and ministry in the city, I know how draining it can be to befriend, love, and relationally commit to people who are wounded and loveless, persecuted, and needy. Tim Keller says in his book *King's Cross,* "It has to be this way because all life-changing love is substitutionary sacrifice."[4] Because of God's love, Jesus made that kind of sacrifice for our messed-up, emotionally troubled lives. Instead of avoiding us, Jesus crossed the biggest cultural divide ever, leaving his heavenly comfort to make the ultimate emotional and physical sacrifice. Jesus taught that if we only love those who love us or are kind only to our friends, what good

4. Keller, *King's Cross,* 141.

is that and how are we different from people who don't believe in Christ (Matt 5:46–47)?

Crossing culture and being multiracial is becoming popular in our Western society. From commercials to celebrities, we are bombarded with multiethnic images of unity. These are all positive pictures but are devoid of a story behind the faces. How often we would host well-meaning white suburbanites in our "hood" for a weekend, who couldn't wait to take pictures with our neighbors without getting to know their story. Reynolds Chapman from the Duke Center for Reconciliation reportedly said, "It's like skipping to the climax of a movie without watching the ninety minutes that lead up to it." Crossing culture's substitutionary sacrifice requires a patient long-term commitment to know, love, and submit to those who are not only different from us but whose needs may cost us something as their troubles and issues become ours. As Keller writes, "You can't love them without taking a hit yourself. A transfer of some kind is required."[5]

Developing a two-way cultural bridge and finding the common ground with other cultures is furthered challenged by a temptation to overadapt to our own culture. The three -isms of materialism, individualism, and pragmatism contribute to an entrenchment in a cultural idolatry. We want just enough material goods to make life comfortable. We believe God is in charge of the universe, but individually, we prefer to be in control of our part of the world. And we may not be right about some things, but pragmatically, we prefer to do what conveniently works for us. The idols of comfort, control, and convenience, coupled with our membership in the white majority, slow the progress of bridge building. Tim Keller writes in his book *Center Church:* "If we need the approval of the receiving culture too much, we will compromise in order to be liked. If we are too proudly rooted in any one culture, we will be rigid and unable to adapt. Only the gospel gives us the balance we need. The gospel makes us both humble and

---

5. Keller, *King's Cross*, 141.

confident at once; these two attitudes are critical for doing faithful and sound contextualization."[6]

Paul used the gospel when he confronted Peter's failure to continue fellowship with gentile believers, accusing him of not walking in line with the gospel. Faith in the gospel gives us the humility and confidence we need to shift our cultural clothing temporarily in order to bridge the cultural divides. It also keeps us from retreating in the face of rejection or attempting to deny our cultural blunders.

On more than one occasion, in my desire to be accepted by our African American community, I looked past some behaviors and shortcomings in a couple of our Black leaders. Some mature Black congregants pulled me aside to challenge me in my blind spot. I was not applying the standards of the gospel equally. A similar situation happened in our mentoring program when it was pointed out that some of our white mentors were lowering the expectations for our Black students. One Black educator in our church said we were crippling these children by coddling them and expecting they were unable to learn. It became apparent to me there was a subtle pride in our white culture and a compromise of sorts in order to be accepted by the Black community. We had created a one-way cultural bridge and had undermined the gospel in the process.

In another circumstance, our church had grown to about 80 percent capacity in our sanctuary. Church development strategies suggest that you will not grow beyond those numbers, and it is either time to start a second service or find a larger facility. Our leadership had begun some brief discussions about what a second service would look like or how we could accommodate more people in our present service. Unbeknownst to me, a group of our white leaders had begun to meet for prayer and discussions about what to do with our crowded Sunday mornings. That ended with a decision on their part that the church needed to move to the near suburbs. At our next leadership meeting, the debate clearly broke down along racial lines. When I pointed this out, the few Black

6. Keller, *Center Church*, 116.

leaders felt patronized when the majority leaders assured them that leaving their neighborhood was not a racial issue. It seemed like the decision had been made, and in a purely reactionary moment, I resigned out of anger and frustration. The next morning while I was on the phone with some denominational leaders, my wife began to get phone calls from a few Blacks in our church asking her to tell me that if I quit all the Blacks in the church would leave. Needless to say, after some time of repentance on my part, I didn't leave, the church didn't move, and with the support of our mother church, we continued the mission God had given us for our urban neighborhood. Over the next two years, we went from being a majority white church to about 50 percent African American. It wasn't always easy to learn from these experiences, and the next decade brought more painful setbacks but also joyful advancements in the journey of bridging our cultural divisions.

Here are a few principles I have learned along the way. First, focus on the marginalized over the multitudes. The misfits, the round pegs in the square holes of the dominant culture, see things differently. They are not always fond of customary beliefs or social norms, and sometimes they have little respect for the status quo. People who struggle as minorities, from a lack of power and resources, are much more in tune with the hard realities of life. They know how to overcome disparities and how to live without the safety net of materialism. You can disagree with them, but you can't ignore them, because they know what it will take to change things. They push the envelope of the human race forward. Given the opportunity, they can lead as early adapters and change agents. The multitudes rarely lead; they usually follow.

When Philip reveals to Nathaniel that they have found the promised Messiah and that "his name is Jesus, the son of Joseph from Nazareth," Nathaniel responds, "Can anything good come from Nazareth?" (John 1:45–46). Nathaniel takes his negative view of a place on the other side of the tracks, with its outcast inhabitants, and assumes the Messiah could never come from Nazareth. He doesn't ask if it is possible; he questions whether anything good at all can come from there. John Piper writes concerning

Nathaniel, "If his heart were gracious, loving, patient and hopeful toward the people of Nazareth, he might have been more legitimately skeptical,"[7] but Nathaniel's prejudice nearly caused him to miss the Son of God.

There is much to be learned from those who are on the margins of society. We ran a job training program for ex-offenders. With a substantial grant, we paid for their part-time employment with various businesses, usually as janitors, carpenters, mason tenders, or painters. They were required to attend our classes while working at least twenty hours per week during the six-month program. The hope was that they would be hired full-time or use the experience as leverage to get another job. Our church decided to hire its trainee as a full-time janitor. As I spent time with him and heard his story, from the streets and the penitentiary, I realized how much wisdom he had gleaned from his broken life. As an African American, his friendship and his thoughts on our country's racial tensions were informative and invaluable to me.

What furthers hinders us from embracing and learning from those on society's margins is our obsession with measuring success. We prefer to focus on statistics over getting to know the story of someone's life. It is not just the pastors who get anxious when only twenty-five people show up for worship. Our fixation with numbers has enabled the existence of the contemporary megachurch. We have the management and methodologies to gather a crowd and the technology to analyze our success, but in the process, we can miss people. I dreaded filling out our denomination's annual report that focused on the number of noses and nickels we had gathered. I longed to tell a story of what God was doing in the life of a single person. I wanted to share the stories behind the lives of people who on Sundays would stand up to announce today was the anniversary of their sobriety.

I was meeting with a well-known, long-tenured African American pastor and community leader when I mentioned my position as a board member with a local urban nonprofit. It was an organization that brought suburban youth in for a week or two

---

7. Piper, *Bloodlines*, 221.

to do home renovations for the elderly poor. His response was, "You mean the white plantation." I was taken aback at first, but I soon knew what he meant. This organization was run by well-intentioned white suburban churches whose camp fees paid for their youth to attend this cross-cultural experience and was further supplemented by foundation grants. The counselors were predominantly white college kids, and the local urban community had limited input. Many leaders in Black communities felt that organizations like this were using race and poverty as tools to run their successful-looking outreaches to the inner city. It is why when I was attempting to build a relationship with another Black urban leader, he told me he had to be careful with whom he could partner with and befriend in the white community, so he would not undermine his credibility with his own people. Every year we would recruit mentors for our YES Kids program from a few suburban churches on Sunday mornings, and we were always asked to bring some of our inner city kids along. We refused, as we were not going to use any of our youth as a poster child to enlist tutors for reading and math. And in fairness the ministry where I was a board member gradually turned things around, running a camp for urban youth, hiring non-white counselors, and involving community leadership.

When we first planted our church, I was told by a seasoned urban practitioner that I was wasting my time if I didn't see myself there for at least ten to fifteen years, because that is how long it would take to raise up indigenous leaders from the youth in the neighborhood. Not exactly a recipe for a quick measurement of success or immediate gratification. I stayed nearly twenty years. Bridging the cultural divide cannot be fueled by our desire to look successful.

Many of us may be aware that Matthew's gospel mentions four women with questionable character in his genealogy of the Messiah. Tamar, Rahab, Ruth, and Bathsheba—incestuousness, prostitution, adultery, and all who were well outside the Jewish faith. They were anomalous in their ancestry and, with the exception of Ruth, in their moral character. Yet even Ruth was a Moabite and a descendant of Lot's incestuous relationship with his daughters. These are not exactly the role models parents use to instruct their daughters or the kind of women they would want their sons to marry. It almost appears Matthew has gone out of his way to find women who contaminate Jesus's bloodline, who tarnish his pure Jewish ancestry. People expected the Messiah to come from the pure kingly line of David. Yet, curiously, there is no record in the Gospels of any disputes over Jesus being a descendant of David.

So why didn't Matthew record the more prestigious names of Sarah, Rebecca, and Rachael, the wives of the patriarchs? Because Matthew is preaching the gospel of divine mercy. A gospel that not only comes for sinners but through sinners. A gospel that presents a Savior for all people, a Light for all nations, and a mercy bigger than our sins. A mercy that is bigger than a person's religious affiliations, political leanings, racial makeup, or even idol worship. This is evidenced by Matthew asking us to identify with the pagan wise men from the East, not the reigning political leaders of the time nor the spiritual elite of Jerusalem. No, Matthew's Gospel wants us to identify with the outsiders and their storied history, outsiders in both race and religion.

I was being mentored by a woman who had experience and expertise with an issue where I was doing some special counseling. Knowing that athletics had been and still were a big part of my life, she turned to me one day and told me if I was going to minister in the context of diversity and brokenness, I would need to give up the desire to always win. Sometimes, conviction comes on you gradually over time; this was not one of those times. Conviction struck me like an arrow to the heart. A competitive spirit will eventually dry up a heart of compassion. Demonstrating God's impartiality does not work if you simply try to fit people into accomplishing goals, objectives, and strategies.

For example, if a church analyzes it needs to grow, it might set an objective to increase attendance by 25 percent in two years. Quarterly goals are established, and a strategy is put in place to accomplish those goals. Then people are recruited and trained to carry out specific tactics. The program is reviewed and adjustments are made to meet the stated goals. This is what we used to call management by objectives. While it may still be a good business practice, the problem is, people are not considered until after all goals have been established. People become secondary to reaching the original objective of increasing attendance.

Jesus gives us a better example in his encounter with a Samaritan women (John 4:4–30). Jesus had stopped to rest from his long walk and was sitting next to a well, when a Samaritan woman approaches to draw some water. Without hesitation, Jesus asks the woman for a drink. She is surprised, since Jews would have nothing to do with the half-breed Samaritans. Even with his knowledge of her multiple marriages, Jesus has compassion and sensitivity for the woman, bridging the cultural gap and opening the door for communication. They discuss her perceived physical need for water that allows Jesus to help her discover a deeper spiritual need for living water. Throughout the entire conversation, Jesus treats her with love and respect, enabling her to emerge with a sense of personal dignity and confidence, with her particular history and her newly discovered longings for what Jesus had to offer. Nothing is more attractive then knowing someone genuinely cares about you, regardless of your questionable past or your lack of social acceptance—unlike the disciples, who were shocked that Jesus would have an encounter with such a disreputable woman, resembling the racial and sexual prejudices of their world at large.

The object of the comparison between Jesus and a management by objectives approach is to point out where people enter into the action and how differently we treat them. The woman at the well is brought into the process right from the start. Jesus's empathy and warmth for the woman, over a strategic analysis to assure his success, allowed him to get to know the woman's story. Often, unknowingly, in our attempts to cross the ethnic, racial, and social barriers, we approach people as projects or as a person to be fixed, rather than as God's image bearer to be known and loved.

If we will allow a compassion for the stories of the marginalized to be a priority over our competition for the statistics of the multitudes, we can begin to bridge the cultural divide. It might require standing alone, but it will bear witness to the glory of God's impartiality.

Chapter 7

Becoming Third-Culture People

IN THEIR BOOK *NEXT Door as It Is in Heaven*, authors Lance Ford and Brad Briscoe discuss the profound loneliness people are regularly experiencing in our world and the subsequent sense that they have very little value at all. This was especially true during the recent pandemic. Sadly, many of us contribute to this loneliness and lack of self-worth as we move throughout our day, rarely even lifting our heads to offer a simple greeting. This is all the more real when we encounter someone outside our group. Ford and Briscoe contrast our relational aloofness with the daily practice author Peter Senge noticed among the tribes of northern Natal in South Africa: "The most common greeting, equivalent to 'hello' in English, is the expression: Sawu bona. It literally means, 'I see you.' If you are a member of the tribe, you might reply by saying Sikhona, 'I am here.' The order of the exchange is important: until you see me, I do not exist. It's as if, when you see me, you bring me into existence." Ford and Briscoe further observe: "A deep truth resides in this cultural practice. When we merely move throughout our days without seeing people as people, then as far as it matters to us in that moment, they really don't exist. . . . [But] being conscious of how we approach people we encounter through the normal routines of our day is a step toward bringing . . . heaven here on our patch of earth."[1]

This is in part what I believe it means to become third-culture people: approaching people who feel like lonely outsiders with our impartiality and offering a little slice of heaven on earth. This requires us to be heavenly minded as well as being some earthly good. It calls for leaving the comfort and familiarity of our homogeneity to welcome and embrace the other, those outside our race and social bubble. Author and pastor Bryan Loritts says third-culture people are "culturally flexible and adaptable without becoming ethnically ambiguous or hostile. They have a wide range of relationships and navigate various ethnicities and culture while maintaining their unique identity."[2] In other words, we can embrace differences without losing who we are.

Miroslav Volf offers a wonderful picture of such an embrace as a double movement of opening and closing. First, an opening of the arms to create space for the other and an invitation to be inclusive. Then, a brief moment of patience for a reciprocal closure of the arms. Volf warns, however, to not close the arms too tightly, "so as to crush her and assimilate her, otherwise I will be engaged in a concealed power-act of of exclusion."[3] We must be careful to not allow our lifestyle preferences to dominate the relationship of someone from a different background. Third-culture people have the ability to do this model embrace, because they are secure in their own identity and have a healthy understanding of what it means to be the other. Authors Pollock and Van Reken offer additional insight in their book about third-culture kids, who are neither like the culture in which the parents originated nor the culture from where the family currently resides but more like a blend of the two.[4] These children integrate aspects of their birth environment with their new surroundings and lifestyle, creating

---

1. Ford and Briscoe, *Next Door*, 76.

2. Loritts, *Right Color, Wrong Culture*, 201.

3. Volf, *Exclusion and Embrace*, 143.

4. Pollock and Van Reken, *Third Culture Kids*.

a unique third culture, giving them the ability to relate to others much more than those who come from either of their two cultures.

As Christians, we are an amalgamation of two cultures: the kingdom of this world and the kingdom of heaven. We are residents of the world in which we live, still familiar with its patterns, customs, and behaviors, but our citizenship is in heaven. This means we have two callings. We are called to a certain worldliness, having been sent into the world to get involved in the culture around us (John 17:15, 17), and we are also called to be holy. "You must be holy . . . just as God who chose you is holy" (1 Pet 1:15).

Peter's first epistle uses the term alien to best describe this dual calling, this synthesis of cultures and this role of being third-culture people. It is a term used throughout Scripture, from Abraham's calling to leave his homeland to Jesus's mission and ultimate rejection. Jesus was alien to the world, because the world he entered was estranged from God. The term alien implies a distance in relationship to a culture's values and ideals, a distance from the prevailing social environment.[5] Before conversion, Peter's community was much like their unbelieving neighbors, but after committing to Christ, they became different, and this was the cause of the discrimination and persecution they faced (1 Pet 4:4). They were at one time alienated from God, then they became distanced from the culture in which they lived. This distance, caused by the new birth, was twofold. It distanced them from their old way of life inherited from their ancestors, and it distanced them from the culture's outlook on life in the future. The culture's view of the future was death; the Petrine community's view was now eternal life.

When I say distance, I don't mean in space and time. I mean that the new birth, becoming a Christian, is not *living* like you used to live and not *being* who you used to be, and that creates a distance from the way the prevailing culture lives. Imagine a foreigner visits this country, you fall in love with each other and you marry. But you adopt the nationality and the customs of the foreigner you married while still living in this country. In fact, you are no longer a citizen of your own country but rather a resident

5. Volf, "Soft Difference," 16ff.

alien. How difficult would it be to give up your old way of life, your customs, and traditions, and still live here? Peter makes the point that Jesus came from heaven to earth; married us, his bride the church; and asks us to live according to his way of life, even though we continue to live here on earth. We are asked to adopt a heavenly manner of living in the midst of a worldly culture, an alternative way of life within the political, racial, and religious institutions of the larger society. How do we do that when rules and norms encourage us to stay within our homogenous group? How do we bridge the cultural divide if we are distanced, alienated, from relationships in the mainstream mores?

Peter gives two directives: one negative and one positive. "Keep away from evil desires" and "live such good lives" (1 Pet 2:11–12). Do not live as if we are still committed to the habits of this world, but resist the temptations to our old way of life, even though we found them pleasurable. This old nature wars against our new status and our new ruler. However, nowhere are we instructed to mount an assault against the beliefs and practices of others. Rather, we are exhorted to be different based on a holy God and a suffering Christ. The emphasis is on a future hope, not the damnation of others.

Barna research finds that the number one quality non-Christians and lapsed Christians look for when seeking out a person to talk with about faith is "listens without judgment." In addition, a recent Barna survey asked unchurched millennials, ages nineteen to thirty-five, to give one word that for them described present-day Christianity: 87 percent responded with the word "judgmental."[6] Whether reality or perception, the result is the same; Christians are seen as censorious.

Even with the oppression and intolerance Peter's original readers faced, Peter appears less interested in instructing them to hurl threats against aggressive neighbors and more focused on celebrating the identity and special privilege the community has in Christ (1 Pet 3:9). Miroslav Volf says, "Identity can be forged through two related but clearly distinctive processes: either

6. Barna Group, "Millenials at Church."

through a negative process of rejecting the beliefs and practices of others or through a positive process of giving allegiance to something distinctive."[7] In other words, we can be known either by what we oppose and fight against or by what we favor and the way we live. The injunction is not "don't be as your neighbors are" but rather "don't be as you were."

This leads to Peter's second directive of behaving honorably or living such good lives. We are to live the kind of good life that our neighbors may see it and give honor to God. The good here is a word that describes something attractive and appreciated by others. The emphasis is on the manner in which we do good and our consistency—doing good over the long haul. When we first moved into our present city, we met the head of the local neighborhood group. He lived a very different lifestyle from us, but he loved Christians who moved into the community because, in his opinion, they improved and maintained their homes, as well as obeyed the laws. That was the common good we had with him, and it enabled us to establish a friendship with someone outside our cultural norms and outside our faith community. It also gave us the opportunity to talk to him about our Christian worldview.

When the Susan B. Anthony dollar was introduced, it didn't take long for it to fail, because it was hard to distinguish it from a quarter. This is why Peter says be careful how you live, so people can distinguish your worth and value from the rest of the world. There should be something special about our good behavior and our good deeds, not necessarily spectacular but simple and inviting, done in humility and without fanfare. The goal of this distinctiveness is to enable us to undertake cultural bridge building. Visible interracial relationships of mutuality become easily distinguishable from the status quo.

However, many of us are what one author calls rabbit hole Christians. In the morning we pop out of our safe home and comfortable surroundings, hold our breath at work, scurry home to our families, then off to our Bible studies, where we pray for all the people we safely avoided all day. Too often, we either embrace the

7. Volf, "Soft Difference," 20.

culture so there is no noticeable difference, or we separate so that the difference becomes a wall of hostility. What the apostle Peter describes is neither an over- or underengagement with culture. Author Nicholas Wolterstorff describes it best when he writes: "It seems to me that the Christian life, when properly lived, is a rhythmic alternation between turning toward God in worship and running toward the world in love and with a passion for justice, between congregation and dispersal, liturgy and labor, worship and work, adoration and obedience."[8]

This is how we live out this strange combination of being distinguished from the world and being acculturated in this world. It is how we show the divergent culture the love of God without using pressure or manipulation. We can do this because we are secure in this living hope, this wonderful expectation of our future. Whether we are persecuted or discriminated against, people see our honorable behavior. Once a citizen of a different kingdom, we were ruled by our insecurities and resulting prejudices, but we left that behind when we chose to submit ourselves to Jesus as our new King. If we love, serve, and fellowship with people, regardless of their racial or cultural heritage, their social or economic status, their political viewpoints, or their religious beliefs, we will begin to reaffirm our identity and purpose in life as third-culture people.

Our identity is complex and multilayered. I am an Anglo-American, Christian pastor with a doctorate, raised in a rural working-class family. These are all parts of who I am. The problem becomes when I begin to assign a higher value to any one component of my identity, expecting it to work for my advantage. If I think my identity should offer me some privilege over someone's race, social status, education, or belief system, then I am revealing an underlying prejudice. To presuppose our race or position in life is superior to another is pernicious and sinful. We then make our cultural preferences into moral absolutes and a badge of self-righteousness, nullifying God's grace in our lives. It ignores the divine truth that all of us have equal dignity and worth based on being created in the image of God. I am aware there have been

8. Wolterstorff, as cited in "Classic and Contemporary Excerpts."

times in my heart when I have felt superior to others based on my identity as an educated white pastor in a working poor Black neighborhood. Thankfully, the gospel transforms our identities over time. I became less concerned about what my peers thought over perceived failures or successes, more open to various political opinions, willing to learn from those who were racially different than me, and more gracious to those who had no faith in Christ.

Richard Lovelace writes, "Once faith is exercised, a Christian is free . . . he is released to admire and appreciate the differing expressions of Christ shining out through other cultures."[9] Even when differing cultural expressions rub against the inclinations of our upbringing and heritage, faith empowers us to respect and embrace those intimations.

During one particular racial incident in our city, I was with a group of Black pastors who were planning to meet with the community to head off any potential violence from hitting the streets. I asked how I could participate and help. I was told pointedly I couldn't. It was a blow to my ego, but I had learned I must respect their reasons for such decisions. It was not the time for an appearance or the voice of a white pastor.

While racial and cultural differences can be used in sinful ways, God has designed those distinctions to edify and enrich the human family. We all have our cultural prejudices, which God can convert, but we also have cultural perspectives that can strengthen our church and community. The challenge is to differentiate between prejudices and perspectives. Author Lamin Sanneh conveys the idea that Christianity does not supersede our cultural identity with some other culture but rather converts it.[10] She points out that African Christians' faith began to grow dramatically when they understood they did not have to become Eurocentric to become Christians. They had to adjust some of their culture to line up with the gospel, but they could still embrace much of their African heritage. God gave them enough distance from their culture to adequately examine it under the light of the gospel.

9. Lovelace, *Dynamics of Spiritual Life*, 199.
10. Sanneh, *Whose Religion Is Christianity?*

To be third-culture people, we must maintain this balance of closeness and critique of our home culture. We do this through love and accountability with others from various racial, ethnic, and social backgrounds. This includes allowing friendships with unbelievers to assess our life of faith. Is our conveyance of faith full of grace and truth, or do we come across as legalistic and hubristic? We become third-culture people by continually creating this two-way bridge of transcultural relationships that both judges and completes who we are.

Those who came to faith in Christ were presented with a gospel outfitted in a set of cultural clothes, but God is not limited to one ensemble. So much of what is done in church—the order and length of worship, music, and preaching styles—are cultural preferences, not scriptural prescriptions. Yet we become wedded to these styles and patterns as the only correct way to be the church. In a similar fashion, we become comfortably attached to our homogeneous group and lifestyle, sometimes secretly looking down on people different in race, class, and politics.

To overcome this prejudicial leaning, our society, young and old, need to see and hear the seasoned and literary lives of third-culture people. They need lives that shatter the stereotypes of prejudices, who will disturb the status quo and challenge preconceived mental pictures of others. Blogger Cindy Brandt writes, "In this fast paced society of sound bites and noise, we need the sharpened clarity brought by multiple cultural lenses."[11] As third-culture people who build bridges with two-way traffic, we can become that cultural lens. Because according to Esau McCaulley, "God's vision for his people is not for the elimination of ethnicity to form a colorblind uniformity of sanctified blandness. Instead God sees the creation of a community of different cultures united by faith in his Son as a manifestation of the expansive nature of his grace."[12]

---

11. Brandt, "Third Culture Kids."

12. McCaulley, *Reading While Black*, 106.

Conclusion

A FEW RESEARCH PSYCHOLOGISTS have looked into the relationship between religiosity and celebrity worship. The team, consisting of researchers from England and the United States, conducted a study in which 307 participants were asked questions that gauged their attitudes toward religion and toward their favorite celebrities. They concluded, "Many religious people apparently ignore the religious teaching that 'Thou shalt worship no other gods,' or fail to connect it to their 'worship' of celebrities."[1] Success is most often defined by achievements, acquisitions, and acclamations and measured by our work, the people we hang out with, and the ones we idolize. I have heard that Tim Keller, speaking at the Action Institute, said, "When you make work your identity . . . if you are successful it destroys you because it goes to your head. If you're not successful it goes to your heart—it destroys your self-worth." It can be similar with people and relationships. When we look at relationships as a measure of our success, they are no longer people created in God's image but pawns in our pursuit for a successful identity. Does success require our relationships to be only with those who are famous, popular, or like us?

Whether it is the history of the world unfolding, or the theology of God's kingdom being shaped, or the daily struggle of our mundane activities, every life of faith is worked out in relationship with others. In every innovation, movement, or vocation, people take up most of our time and energy. We all have a combination

1. Halpern, *Fame Junkies*, 164–65.

of willful enemies, unpredictable acquaintances, and unwavering friends. And whether hidden or public, our life of faith is shaped in the context of such varied relationships. At one time in his life, the prophet Jeremiah had three such relationships.[2]

Jeremiah had been a public figure for over thirty years, speaking truth and agonizing over the fate of Jerusalem. The people, on the other hand, were trying to ignore the reality of God's coming judgment at the hands of the Babylonians. Patriotism was at an all-time high, and loyalty was being confused with morality. Consequently, when Jeremiah attempted to leave the city, Irijah the sentry took the opportunity to show his allegiance by accusing and arresting Jeremiah of defecting to the enemy. Irijah used his position to avoid any moral responsibility, any sense of justice. In his mind, he was just obeying the law, doing what he was told. While Jeremiah protested his innocence, he accepted the stupidity and unfairness of it all. He didn't threaten or curse, he simply endured. Jeremiah had long given up the need to be popular or appear successful, even in the midst of being unjustly imprisoned and beaten.

Most of us would prefer to agree with the philosopher Immanuel Kant, who argued that a person should be loved and forgiven only if he or she deserves it.[3] Let's be honest, it is hard enough to love our brothers and sisters in Christ, much less someone who is an enemy. We all have our enemies, someone who has hurt us, hates us, persecutes us, or just disagrees with us. There are people in our lives whom we have walled off for protection or excluded for the sake of appearances. Yet Jesus gives us an answer as to why we are to love such people: "In that way you will be acting as true children of your Father in heaven" (Matt 5:45). Too often, we identify a person as our antagonist as a cover for avoiding the discomfort we have with that person's race, political views, or lack of status, fearing how he or she might adversely affect the perception of our success.

---

2. Peterson, *Run with the Horses*, 159–66.

3. Kant, as presented in Johnson and Cureton, "Kant's Moral Philosophy."

Jeremiah also encountered Zedekiah, the puppet king of the Babylonians. Eugene Peterson, writing about King Zedekiah, states, "he would do what he was told by anyone who happened to be in the room with him. The man was a marshmallow."[4] Irijah persuaded the king to arrest Jeremiah just as quickly as Jeremiah, in turn, convinced him that he should be moved from his cell to the courtyard. However, Zedekiah's capricious nature would once again land Jeremiah in prison, this time in an empty cistern full of mud. Whether an adversarial opponent or the mercurial temperament of an associate, we are forced to contend with all kinds of relationships, yet we must not be too quick to turn our back on such a spectrum of connections. We never know when some interloper may suddenly become an ally in our time of need.

This was the case for Jeremiah. He may not have been very popular or successful, but he discovered he was not without friends. Ebedmelech, a Cushite, an Ethiopian, a Black man, with no legal standing because he was a eunuch, went to the fickle king and got permission to rescue Jeremiah from the miry pit. This was an unpopular move with those who were not exactly fond of the prophet. It didn't matter to the Cushite. He went and got some rags to put under Jeremiah's arms and, with the help of the king's men, pulled Jeremiah from the well. God used this misfit from the margins to liberate Jeremiah from sinking further into the mud of the cistern.

Life is hard. We are not meant to live a life of self-sufficiency and proud independence. In receiving friendship and help, we most often expose a weakness, admit a defeat, or even confess a sin. In addition, when that help comes from the least, the last, and those left out, it diminishes our résumé of success. My experience has shown me that the people I could count on the quickest to help in an emergency were those who lacked social prominence or rank. Their history of encountering racism and general disfavor towards their lot in life had built in them a dispositional humility. I was continually amazed and humbled by those whom I estimated had the least ability and willingness to come to the aid of others,

4. Peterson, *Run with the Horses*, 163.

yet they were the first to raise their hands or the first to show up. People who had suffered under social injustice or knew what it was like to be in want had the humility to look past the character or color of the person in need. There is research from an article on "Sociodemographic Differences in Humility" that supports my case: "Given that resilience has been linked to greater humility . . . we expect groups in society more likely to experience discrimination or hardship compared to other groups (e.g., women, those with less education, and racial/ethnic minorities) will show greater humility."[5]

Paul agrees with this thinking when he writes, "God chose things despised by the world [or those who are low born], things counted as nothing at all, and used them to bring to nothing what the world considers important" (1 Cor 1:28). God chose the *nobodies* of this world to expose the foolishness and the weakness of the *somebodies*. One of our staunchest supporters and closest friends, speaking to our mother church, confessed he thought initially we were foolish to be starting a church in a economically poor, mixed-race neighborhood of the city. Wisdom and power, the standards for popularity and success, have taken much of our Western Christianity captive. In the process, the gospel has been domesticated and the needs of the poor overlooked. Far from this present picture of our faith, Augustine of Hippo saw his role of a pastor this way: "Disturbers are to be rebuked, the low spirited to be encouraged, the infirm to be supported, objectors confuted, the treacherous guarded against, the unskilled taught, the lazy aroused, the contentious restrained, the haughty repressed, the poor relieved, the oppressed liberated, the good approved, the evil borne with, and all are to be loved!"[6]

Scripture teaches us we are to pay all our debts except the debt of love for others, including our enemies (Rom 13:8). Most of us don't like to be indebted to anyone. We prefer to pay back favors from our friends and exact retribution from our enemies. We want to keep things even with recompense or revenge. But that is the

---

5. Webster et al., "Sociodemographic Differences in Humility."
6. Augustine, as cited in Shelley, "Bishop at Work."

preferred method of the proud, a justice that we control so no one can get the upper hand on us. It is a method that exalts ourselves above God rather than give ourselves away like God. So many of Jesus's parables pointed to this self-giving love: a lovesick father who runs to meet his prodigal son, a landlord who cancels a debt too large for anyone to pay, an employer who pays eleventh-hour workers the same as the first-hour crew, a banquet giver who goes to the highways and byways in search of undeserving guests—all stories of an unnatural self-donation. This self-giving love steps over the need for gratitude and affirmation, it steps over the wounds and wrongs suffered at the hands of our enemies. It embraces and befriends people "from every tribe and language and people and nation" (Rev 5:9), recognizing they all have something to contribute to our welfare and the flourishing of the world.

It is not only the lack of humility and our desire to be seen as successful that keep us from overcoming our prejudices to bridge our cultural divide. We fear the contemporary version of Peter's circumcision party, with the occasional loud but frequently subtle voices of disapproval from our favored group. In today's highly charged disagreements, we rarely position ourselves in one large identifiable category. Rather, we search for those people who are compatible with our political, socioeconomic, and racial views, and then we hunker down with these homogeneous friends. Author and professor William Pannell, in his book *The Coming Race Wars?*, writes, "The problem is that too many white people cannot or will not transcend their own system, or, put another way, cannot wrap flesh around the words they profess."[7] In other words, we don't walk the talk. Jack Ellul further supports this supposition in his book *The Subversion of Christianity* when he writes, "We have to admit that there is an immeasurable distance between all that we read in the Bible and the practice of the church and of Christians."[8]

As Western Christians, we want to put our world into neat little compartments to keep our lives ordered. As an example, we

7. Pannell, *Coming Race Wars*, 125–26.
8. Ellul, *Subversion of Christianity*, 7.

tend to label things either good or bad. While that may be legitimate in some cases, it is an oversimplistic approach to our complicated and broken world. Ron Mitchell writes, "It is rare to hear Christian preachers speaking about the world in terms of good and bad mixed together." He goes on to say, "People are drawn to categorize and stereotype, presumably because this helps them cope with a complicated world."[9] The problem is we end up using the presumptive bad in others and the prideful good in ourselves to justify our favoritism and prejudices, as well as our lack of social concern.

Jesus, in his parable on the wheat and the weeds, teaches that although the enemy sowed the weeds (the bad), the wheat and weed must grow up together; for if the weeds were pulled up, the wheat (the good) may get hurt. Commentator Dale Brunner says this ploy of the enemy is to distract workers from the work in the kingdom by concentrating on the evil. He writes, "If he cannot hinder faith, he can corrupt love."[10] This parable guards the church and us against forming exclusive communities and friendships. If we are to co-exist with evil, how much more should we bridge our present cultural separations? Whether that means forging relationships between Black and white, rich and poor, or political opponents, we must do this challenging work to bring a more holistic picture of God's multiethnic kingdom.

In her conclusion of the book *Restorers of Hope*, Amy Sherman says, "Our church life is impoverished to a degree when it does not reflect the multicultural character of the kingdom of God."[11] It is in the midst of a diversity of cultures and economics that we experience God's grace in ways that may be unfamiliar to us. Blacks in our church overcame their encounters with racism and discrimination by whites to accept and love me as their white pastor. That unmerited favor continues to transform me. In relationships with people different from us, our prejudices are revealed and we are stretched to love those who may not love us

9. Mitchell, *Organic Faith*, 79.

10. Brunner, *Church Book*, 497.

11. Sherman, *Restorers of Hope*, 228.

back. This knowledge becomes a piece of God's threshing floor, where he removes the unproductive chaff in our character.

Walter Brueggeman believes the Bible has two different theologies, and Humberto Alfaro summarizes them as survival and celebration.[12] The first comes from people who suffer from the lack of power and money. Suffering is the key element, because when the suffering is relieved, the theology begins to change. The theology of celebration involves song and gratitude that reflect stability and blessing but comes with the responsibility of management and stewardship. God told Moses he was aware of the people's suffering at the hands of the Egyptians and that he had come to rescue them into a "good land" (Exod 3:7–8). At the reconciliation of Joseph and his brothers, Joseph told them, "God turned into good what you meant for evil. He brought me into this high position I have today so I could save the lives of many people" (Gen 50:20). Brueggemann expresses the engagement of these two systematic biblical views with the term prophetic ministry. He states, "Prophetic ministry seeks to penetrate the numbness . . . to penetrate despair, so that new futures can be believed in and embraced by us."[13] The numbness in the theology of celebration, brought on by materialism and hedonism, can be penetrated by the despair and injustices of the survival theology. Likewise, the praise of stability and blessings, rightly managed, can help free those under the oppression of personal and societal sin. In other words, prophetic ministry is bringing these two antithetical theologies of survival and celebration together to imagine a new reality through the revelation of God, under the power of the Holy Spirit, and in the context of community. At the center of these two theologies is Christ. In the tension of the already and the not yet of God's coming kingdom and the strain of the theology of survival and celebration stand the cross and the resurrection of Jesus the Christ. Brueggemann concludes: "Jesus' concern was, finally, for the joy of the kingdom. That is what he promised and into that he invited

---

12. Alfaro, "Pastoral Care and Ministry."

13. Brueggemann, *Prophetic Imagination*, 111.

people. But he was clear that the rejoicing in that future required grieving about the present order."[14]

To overcome playing favorites or having outright prejudices, we need to mourn the present cultural divisions in the world. We cannot change everything we face, but nothing can be changed unless we address it head on. It is time for those of us in the majority culture to make a sane estimate of our attitudes towards race and class, to be "quick to listen, slow to speak" (James 1:19). The dominate Anglo approach is to quickly object or become defensive over any suggestions of prejudicial attitudes or actions. Proverbs 18:13 warns us, "Spouting off before listening to the facts is both shameful and foolish."

Psychologists have found an intriguing way to study what it is that we really like and dislike. It's called "affective priming." They print a word over a bouncing dot on a computer screen. If people's response is positive, they push any key with their left hand; if negative, any key with their right. To discover our deeper responses, researchers will use subliminal stimulation. They'll print a negative word (like "fear" or "storm") subliminally, below your level of awareness. Your intuitive system is so fast it reads those words and responds to them before you are aware. So if they show a negative word subliminally, then a positive word slowly, it takes you longer to move toward a positive response. Sometimes they will flash a subliminal picture instead of a word. When it is a picture of an African American, "Americans of all ages, classes, and political affiliations react with a flash of negativity." Including people who report they have no prejudice at all.[15]

Martin Luther King said, "An individual has not started living until he can rise above the narrow confines of his individualistic concerns to the broader concerns of all humanity."[16] This seems like a simple truth, yet with the rise of nationalism, the continuation of discrimination, and the lack of sensitivity towards refugees, King's statement is just as significant now as it was then.

---

14. Brueggemann, *Prophetic Imagination*, 112.

15. Fazio, "On the Automatic Activation," 116.

16. King, "Birth of a New Age."

Is the Revelation 7:9 vision of God's future kingdom, with "every nation and tribe and people and language," being seen? Is bridging the cultural divide viewed as optional or pursued as a biblical mandate? As Christians, we are called to be rightly related to God and to one another, beyond a polite courtesy and a political correctness towards those different than us.

One of the primary and most important ways Christians can embody the gospel and make the kingdom of God visible is to be connected with those who are racially, ethnically, and culturally different from us. The main objection that postmodern people have with Christianity is the way in which we exclude both other Christians and non-believers who are outside our favorite and dominate group. Consequently, we must be united with outsider Christians and embrace outsider non-Christians.

In Ephesians 2:19–22, Paul teaches us that our relationship to each other in Christ is to be stronger than our relationship to other members of our narrow uniform group. We are not primarily Anglo, African American, Asian, or Latino; nor are we primarily white Presbyterians or Black Baptists, suburbanites or urbanites, Democrats or Republicans. We are citizens of Jesus's kingdom, children of God's family, and stones of the holy temple. Notice how Paul intensifies our identity and draws us closer to the triune God. We are citizens through a social contract with Jesus our King, we are family through a genetic code with God our Father, and we are living stones though a bonding cement with our Holy Spirit. These metaphors all contribute to the picture of our new humanity, a new way of being human beings together. It is this new humanity that then enables us to unite with other Christians who are ethnically, racially, and socioeconomically set apart from us. But Jesus also taught that we show the uniqueness of our Christian faith when we follow his lead to embrace the moral and spiritual outsider (Matt 5:47). We must be willing to give ourselves and make space for unbelievers, especially those who may be culturally different. Embracing outsider non-Christians demonstrates the gospel of grace and reveals that the good news of Christ is open to all who are often considered excluded.

Being third-culture people and bridging the cultural divide involves uniting with the racially foreign and the socially outcast Christian, as well as embracing the dissenting and unbelieving misfit with the gospel of grace. We must increase and deepen these diverse friendships with people we would otherwise not take the time to know. This unity in diversity is not only the result of living out the gospel; it is the most significant way to communicate the gospel. When we do this, we reveal that God's character shows no favoritism, that Jesus broke down the dividing walls of hostility, that God's coming kingdom is multicultural, and we demonstrate what it really means to love our neighbor without playing favorites.

Finally, here are some additional suggestions for overcoming our prejudices to bridge the cultural divide:

1. Make prayer your number one strategic action. Godly heart transformation never takes place without it. Make sure your prayers are first and foremost for *your* transformation, not for those other people outside your group.

2. Take your education into your own hands. Begin reading books, magazines, and journals that deal with current events from the perspective of people from different races, ethnicities, and cultures; do the same with websites, movies, newspapers, music, conferences, and conversations.

3. Seek out someone from whom to learn. Books and things can be a subtle diversion from true transformation, which God usually directs through a person, like iron sharpening iron. Relationships are the ultimate objective, taking the posture of learner and not teacher.

4. Submit yourself to the hands of service providers of a different race and/or ethnicity than your own. Choose a Black doctor for a checkup, an Asian dentist for a cleaning, a Latino auto mechanic for a tune-up, etc. Most racial/ethnic minorities don't have a choice but to submit their intimate, private concerns to white male and female professionals. They must learn to trust whites in such vulnerable matters.

5. Be willing to put yourself in a minority-status. Go to places, events, activities, and functions, becoming a member or regular visitor somewhere where you can be exposed to the cultural and social nuances of other races or ethnicities. Most Blacks or Asians can't hide, even if they try, as their conspicuous features make them targets for staring or looks when in different social contexts. Stick it out as an ongoing practice and keep a detailed journal of these experiences, feelings, and lessons. Determine which experiences you'll establish as an ongoing lifestyle. Remember, these experiments aren't for you to complete a project or to gain knowledge but rather for the purpose of transforming your life.

Small Group Discussion Questions

Introduction

1. What does Paul mean by regarding someone from a "worldly point of view" (2 Cor 5:16)?

2. How can you consider others better than yourself when you believe you are better than they are (Phil 2:3)?

3. Whom have you excluded from your life because of your unforgiveness?

Chapter 1

1. Can you give an example where it feels or appears like God does show favoritism (Rom 2:11)?

2. Why does James say that showing favoritism is a sin (Jas 2:9)?

3. Why is discriminating the same as being double minded (Jas 1:6)?

Chapter 2

1. What are the differences between Hitler's idea of a super race and Paul's picture of one body (Eph 2:14–18)?

2. What were the dividing walls of hostility that Jesus broke down?

3. How have you erected fences around your heart towards those who are different from you?

Chapter 3

1. If you had been one of the first people hired, how would you feel about the landowner's wage system (Matt 20:1–16)?

2. Who would you say are the lepers and who are the gentiles in our society today?

3. What are the determining factors for you in picking sides in an argument over racial or cultural issues?

Chapter 4

1. Give an example when you succumbed to peer pressure.

2. Describe a time when you felt you had to assimilate into a group in order to be accepted (Gal 2:12).

3. Recall a story when you spoke up against a racial bias or injustice within your dominant peer group or a time when you were too afraid to do so.

Chapter 5

1. Explain a time when you attempted to find an escape or exception for not following Scripture.

2. Describe an incident where you purposely avoided getting involved because it would have been too costly or time consuming (Luke 10:25–37).

3. Share a time when you felt excluded or felt like an outsider.

Chapter 6

1. Explain why you sometimes feel superior when helping someone with a burden too heavy for them to overcome (Gal 6:1–5).

2. Describe a disappointment when, after you had helped someone, that person's lack of achievement or appreciation fell short of your expectations.

3. Recall a time when you stopped doing a project or slowed your hurried life to listen to the story of someone different from you.

Chapter 7

1. What does it look like for *you* to become a third-culture person?

2. Are you more known for what you oppose and fight against or by what you favor and the way you live? Explain.

3. Describe a time when you had to submit to a person of another race or ethnicity.

Conclusion

1. In what ways might you harm the church or your community with your premature judgments of others?

2. Is bridging the cultural divide still an option, or is it now a biblical mandate for you? Explain.

3. With which one or two suggestions for overcoming your prejudice can you start now?

Bibliography

Alfaro, Humberto. "Pastoral Care and Ministry in the Urban Setting." Lecture given at Gordon-Conwell Theological Seminary, South Hamilton, MA, June 2003.

Amodio, David. "The Neuroscience of Prejudice and Stereotyping." *Nature Reviews Neuroscience* 15 (Sept. 2014) 1–14. www.researchgate.net/publication/265345113.

Barna Group. *Beyond Diversity: What the Future of Racial Justice Will Require of U.S. Churches.* Ventura, CA: Barna Group Inc., 2021.

———. "Millenials at Church: What Millenials Want When They Visit Church." Barna, Mar. 4, 2015. https://www.barna.com/research/what-millennials-want-when-they-visit-church/.

Bonhoeffer, Dietrich. *The Cost of Discipleship.* Translated by R. H. Fuller, revised by Irmgard Booth. New York: Touchstone, 1995.

Brandt, Cindy. "Third Culture Kids in the World of Faith." *A Life Overseas*, Apr. 7, 2014. https://www.alifeoverseas.com/third-culture-kids-in-the-world-of-faith/.

Brueggemann, Walter. *The Prophetic Imagination.* Philadelphia: Fortress, 1978.

Brunner, F. Dale. *The Christ Book.* Vol. 1 of *Matthew.* Dallas: Word, 1987.

———. *The Church Book.* Vol. 2 of *Matthew.* Dallas: Word, 1987.

Carson, D. A. *Biblical Interpretation and the Church: Text and Context.* Carlisle, UK: Paternoster, 1984.

Casmir, Fred L., ed. *Ethics in Intercultural and International Communication.* Mahwah, NJ: Lawrence Erlbaum, 1997.

Christerson, Brad, et al. *Against All Odds: The Struggle for Racial Integration in Religious Organizations.* New York: New York University Press, 2005.

"Classic and Contemporary Excerpts from August 07, 1987." *Christianity Today.* https://www.christianitytoday.com/ct/1987/august-7/reflections-classic-and-contemporary-excerpts.html.

Di Cintio, Marcello. *Walls: Travels along the Barricades.* New York: Soft Skull, 2013.

Ellul, Jacques. *The Subversion of Christianity.* Translated by Geoffrey W. Bromiley. Grand Rapids: Eerdmans, 1986.

Emerson, Michael. "Released! New Stats on Multiracial Churches." *Mosaix Network Newsletter*, 2019. https://us1.campaign-archive.com/?u=1d74bb 6d7340785b4cb4d127e&id=cb4fdcf119.

Fazio, Russel H. "On the Automatic Activation of Associated Evaluations: An Overview." *Cognition and Emotion* 15, no. 2 (2001) 115–41.

Ford, Lance, and Brad Briscoe. *Next Door as It Is in Heaven: Living Out God's Kingdom in Your Neighborhood*. Carol Stream, IL: NavPress, 2016.

Halpern, Jake. *Fame Junkies: The Hidden Truths behind America's Favorite Addiction*. Boston: Houghton Mifflin Harcourt, 2008.

Hanson, Paul. *The People Called: The Growth of Community in the Bible*. New York: Harper & Row, 1986.

Hoyer, Stephen, and Patrice McDaniel. "From Jericho to Jerusalem: The Good Samaritan From a Different Direction." *Journal of Psychology and Theology* (1990) 329–32.

Inskeep, Steve, host. "Study: NFL Referees Influenced By Coaches' and Players' Sideline Yelling." *NPR*, Nov. 3, 2016. https://www.npr.org/2016/11/03/500480083/study-nfl-referees-a-influenced-by-coaches-and-players-sideline-yelling.

Johnson, Robert, and Adam Cureton, "Kant's Moral Philosophy." Stanford Encyclopedia of Philosophy Archive, Spring 2021; first published Feb. 23, 2004; revised July 7, 2016. https://plato.stanford.edu/archives/spr2021/entries/kant-moral/.

Keller, Timothy. *Center Church: Doing Balanced, Gospel-Centered Ministry in Your City*. Grand Rapids: Zondervan, 2012.

———. *King's Cross: The Story of the World in the Life of Jesus*. New York: Dutton, 2011.

Kierkegaard, Søren. "Followers, Not Admirers." In *Bread and Wine*, 55–60. Walden, NY: Plough, 2003.

King, Martin Luther, Jr. "'The Birth of a New Age,' Address Delivered on 11 August 1956 at the Fiftieth Anniversary of Alpha Phi Alpha in Buffalo." Stanford University: The Martin Luther King Jr. Research and Education Institute. https://kinginstitute.stanford.edu/king-papers/documents/birth-new-age-address-delivered-11-august-1956-fiftieth-anniversary-alpha-phi.

———. "'I Have a Dream' Speech, in Its Entirety." *NPR*, delivered Aug. 28, 1963; aired Jan. 18, 2010. https://www.npr.org/2010/01/18/122701268/i-have-a-dream-speech-in-its-entirety.

———. "Transformed Nonconformist." Stanford University: The Martin Luther King Jr. Research and Education Institute, c. Nov. 1–30, 1954. https://kinginstitute.stanford.edu/king-papers/documents/transformed-nonconformist.

Kinder, Donald M., and Lynn M. Sanders. *Divided by Color: Racial Politics and Democratic Ideals*. Chicago: University of Chicago Press, 1996.

Law, Eric H. F. *The Wolf Shall Dwell with the Lamb: Spirituality for Leadership in a Multicultural Community*. St. Louis: Chalis, 1993.

Lee, Sophia. "Leaving Hate Behind." *World Magazine*, Aug. 1, 2019. https://wng.org/articles/leaving-hate-behind-1620615125.

Lindstrom, Martin. *Brandwashed: Tricks Companies Use to Manipulate Our Minds and Persuade Us to Buy*. New York: Crown Business, 2011.

Lints, Richard. *The Fabric of Theology: A Prolegomenon to Evangelical Theology*. Grand Rapids: Eerdmans, 1993.

Loritts, Bryan. *Right Color, Wrong Culture: The Type of Leader Your Organization Needs to Become Multiethnic*. Chicago: Moody, 2014.

Lovelace, Richard F. *Dynamics of Spiritual Life: An Evangelical Theology of Renewal*. Downers Grove, IL: InterVarsity, 1979.

McCaulley, Esau. *Reading While Black: African American Biblical Interpretation as an Exercise in Hope*. Downers Grove, IL: InterVarsity Academic, 2020.

McClesky, Clayton M. "Accentuating Bias." *Wall Street Journal*, Oct. 10, 2010.

McNeil, Brenda Salter, and Rick Richardson. *The Heart of Racial Justice: How Soul Change Leads to Social Change*. Downers Grove, IL: InterVarsity, 2004.

Mitchell, Ron. *Organic Faith: A Call to Authentic Christianity*. Chicago: Cornerstone, 1998.

Morgan, Elisa. *The Beauty of Broken: My Story and Likely Yours Too*. Nashville: Nelson, 2013.

Ortberg, John. "Our Tendency to Exclude." *Preaching Today*, May 2003. https://www.preachingtoday.com/illustrations/2003/may/14407.html?utm_medium=widgetemail.

Palmer, Parker J. *The Company of Strangers: Christians and the Renewal of America's Public Life*. New York: Crossroad,1981.

Pannell, William E. *The Coming Race Wars?: A Cry for Reconciliation*. Grand Rapids: Zondervan, 1993.

Perman, Matt. "Business: A Sequel to the Parable of the Good Samaritan." *Institute for Faith, Work and Economics*, Nov. 1, 2013. https://tifwe.org/business-a-sequel-to-the-parable-of-the-good-samaritan/.

Peterson, Eugene H. *Run with the Horses: The Quest for Life at Its Best*. Downers Grove, IL: InterVarsity, 1983.

Piper, John. *Bloodlines: Race, Cross, and the Christian*. Wheaton, IL: Crossway, 2011.

Pollock, David C., and Ruth E. Van Reken. *Third Culture Kids: Growing Up among Worlds*. Rev. ed. Boston: Nicholas Brealy, 2009.

Redford, Robert, dir. *A River Runs through It*. Culver City, CA: Columbia, 1992.

Religious Herald. "Tony Campolo to Baptists: 'Rise Up, You Suckers, and Do the Work of Jesus.'" *Baptist News Global*, Feb. 20, 2008. https://baptistnews.com/article/tonycampolotobaptistsriseupyousuckersanddotheworkofjesus/#.YWSM_C-B10Q.

Robinson, Haddon. "A Case Study of a Mugging." *Preaching Today*, July 2010. https://www.preachingtoday.com/sermons/sermons/2010/july/acasestudyofamugging.html.

Roets, Arne, and Alain Van Hiel. "Allport's Prejudiced Personality Today: Need for Closure as the Motivated Cognitive Basis of Prejudice." *Current Directions in Psychological Science* 20, no. 6 (2011) 349–54.

Sandburg, Carl. *The People, Yes*. San Diego: Harcourt, 1936.

Sanneh, Lamin. *Whose Religion Is Christianity?: The Gospel beyond the West*. Grand Rapids: Eerdmans, 2003.

Sherman, Amy L. *Restorers of Hope: Reaching the Poor in Your Community with Church-Based Ministries That Work*. Wheaton, IL: Crossway, 1997.

Shelley, Bruce L. "The Bishop at Work." *Christianity Today*, July 1, 2000. https://www.christianitytoday.com/history/issues/issue-67/bishop-at-work.html.

Smith, William. *Smith's Bible Dictionary*. Ada, MI: Revell, 1967.

Thielemann, Bruce. "Hark! the Herald Angels." *Preaching Today*, Aug. 2005. https://www.preachingtoday.com/sermons/sermons/2005/august/063.html.

Volf, Miroslav. *Exclusion and Embrace, A Theological Exploration of Identity, Otherness, and Reconciliation*. Nashville: Abingdon Press, 1996.

———. "Soft Difference: Theological Reflections on the Relation between Church and Culture in 1 Peter." *Ex Auditu* 10 (1994) 15–30.

Webster, Douglas D. *Finding Spiritual Direction: The Challenge and Joys of Christian Growth*. Downers Grove, IL: InterVarsity, 1991.

Webster, Noah J., et al. "Sociodemographic Differences in Humility: The Role of Social Relations." *Research in Human Development* 15, no. 1 (2018) 50–71.

Wilson, Edward O. *The Social Conquest of Earth*. New York: Norton, 2012.

Yancey, Philip. "Denominational Diagnostics." *Christianity Today*, Nov. 19, 2008. https://www.christianitytoday.com/ct/2008/november/27.119.html.

www.ingramcontent.com/pod-product-compliance
Lightning Source LLC
Chambersburg PA
CBHW060311100426
42812CB00003B/735